CONTENTS

UNBREAKABLE

UNBREAKABLE

The trailblazing SAS soldier
who never backed down

MELVYN DOWNES

EBURY
SPOTLIGHT

EBURY SPOTLIGHT

UK | USA | Canada | Ireland | Australia
India | New Zealand | South Africa

Ebury Spotlight is part of the Penguin Random House group of companies whose
addresses can be found at global.penguinrandomhouse.com

Penguin Random House UK
One Embassy Gardens, 8 Viaduct Gardens, London SW11 7BW

penguin.co.uk
global.penguinrandomhouse.com

Penguin
Random House
UK

First published by Ebury Spotlight in 2025

2

Typeset by seagull.net

Printed and bound in Great Britain by Clays Ltd, Elcograf S.p.A.

The authorised representative in the EEA is Penguin Random House Ireland,
Morrison Chambers, 32 Nassau Street, Dublin D02 YH68.

A CIP catalogue record for this book is available from the British Library

Hardback ISBN 9781529961096
Trade Paperback ISBN 9781529969375

MIX
Paper | Supporting
responsible forestry
FSC® C018179

Penguin Random House is committed to a sustainable future
for our business, our readers and our planet. This book is
made from Forest Stewardship Council® certified paper.

To my wife, Zoe, and kids, Amy and Sam

FOREWORD
BILLY BILLINGHAM

You think you know a bloke.

You fight alongside each other for years. You sit across from each other in the mess. You have nights out drinking. You appear on the same bloody television show. Then you read their book and realise that in lots of ways you didn't really know them at all.

It's funny that one of the biggest talkers I know, a man who loves to chat, would be silent about so much that has shaped his life. He never really told us about the racist abuse he suffered when he was a kid at school, or the way that he's taken constant inspiration from the example set by his parents. We were there for him when he was going through his darkest emotional struggles, but I don't think he ever really let on how far he almost fell.

Still, I've been lucky enough to watch him at work and play for over 30 years, so there's a lot in the book that didn't come as a surprise.

Like a lot of the blokes in the regiment, Mel's had to graft for anything good that's come in his life. He's also had as many dances with death as anyone else I know. I reckon what's got him through it is his mindset. Mel's relentlessly positive and totally resilient. He's able to make the best of any situation because he's learned that whether you're a special forces operator or an accountant, at some point life's going to throw a whole load of nonsense in your face. And then, just when you think you're safe, it'll do it all over again.

You can't stop that happening. What you *are* in control of is how you react. If you're like Mel, you'll take a moment, flash the world a smile, then roll your sleeves up and get to work.

The other thing that I think shines through in this book is Mel's unshakeable integrity. That's one of the reasons he thrived from the first moment he stepped through the doors at Hereford. He's a stand-up bloke, always the first to offer to take responsibility, the first to put his hand up when he knows he's messed up, the first to put himself forward when one of his mates needs help.

The nature of our work means that only a very tiny number of people will ever hear the truth about what the SAS have done and continue to do in the service of our country. We knew about that secrecy when we signed up, so none of us could, or would ever want to, complain about the discretion we all have to show. So there's a lot Mel has had to keep under his hat. He'll take a lot of those things to his grave.

Still, Mel's book is as good as anything out there at taking you right to the heart of battle. His long career before joining the SAS and the years he spent protecting journalists in some of the world's most dangerous places mean there's no shortage of action to choose from. (I can't believe the lunatic volunteered to go to Baghdad with little more to protect him than a pistol and body armour that barely covered his T-shirt! Even harder to believe: he lived to tell the tale.) Reading it transported me to my own experiences in combat. It's there in his recall of tiny details. The noise bullets make as they ping off the outside of an APC. The smell that rises from men struggling to conquer their fear. The sheer weirdness of fighting in the unnatural green glow shone by our night-vision goggles. The sickening feeling that comes when one of your mates is hit.

He's honest about the ways in which these things have impacted him. Like so many who've spent so much time in uniform, he's still fighting a lot of ghosts from his past. I really respect his willingness to open up and talk with brutal honesty about the challenges these have presented to his mental health. I'm sure this will help others, from every walk of life, to do the same. Knowing Mel, he'd be delighted with that.

It probably sounds like a bit of a cliché but I don't really care. Mel is one of the good guys. A modest bloke with a hell of a lot to boast about. He's written an amazing book that I hope he's proud of. He should be.

PROLOGUE
NOTHING ELSE MATTERS

All I want to do is get out. I hate doing this. I don't like being so high up, I don't like being burdened by so much gear.

I'm in the hold of a shuddering, rumbling transport plane, thousands of feet above solid ground. The journey is conducted in semi-darkness. Even on night missions the lights are kept low, to ensure that we're not shocked by the transition into the dark skies outside.

With everyone and all their weapons and kit in, what had seemed like a gaping space begins to feel claustrophobic. Some of us are even sitting on our packs. Others are on the floor, their knees up by their chins.

All around us is the reek of engine fuel. But as we get closer to our destination, I can smell something else: adrenaline rising from other men's bodies; steadily increasing nervous energy. There is barely an inch to move in. When I feel too cramped, I try to stretch, lifting my legs up into the empty air above us – there is nowhere else for them to go. More than anything, I am desperate for fresh air.

The hours before a mission are always strange. Occasionally we will get updates through our radios. Otherwise, we are left to our own devices. Some of us put headphones on – when I need to get myself in the right frame of mind, I'll blast out 'Paint It Black' by the Rolling Stones or 'Live Forever' by Oasis. We often talk about football, or other subjects that have no connection to what we are about to do. We know there is nothing we can do except wait, so we just chat about life, take the piss out of each other. It's not until the last few minutes, when we know we will soon get the signal to move, that this changes.

But today none of this is possible. It's so loud inside that we must shout to make ourselves heard, even when talking to the man sitting directly beside us. So we all retreat inside our own heads.

I look around and see blokes with their faces daubed in camouflage paint. We're all swaddled in layers of clothing as a protection from the cold that increases as we climb higher and higher into the air. But to begin with, we're all uncomfortably hot: sweat is already pooling beneath my fatigues and the body armour that encases me front and back.

For a few moments my mind drifts away from what we're about to do. I have been a soldier all my adult life. First with the Staffordshire Regiment, then with the SAS. There are times when I think about all of the things I have done and seen, all the places I have been to, all the times I have been in combat, and feel a kind of vertigo: did all of this really happen?

Those experiences can blur into one. But at other moments, like now, fragments from these events return to me with almost painful clarity. *The way the face of a man who I had just killed in close combat changed instantly. His skin had been pink from heat and exertion, then all the colour simply disappeared. He was ghost-pale. Though everything had happened incredibly quickly, it did not feel that way to me. Time slowed down to a sludgy crawl. My senses became almost ferally acute. I felt assailed by the stench of blood, sweat, gun oil and fear.*

The time when, once, behind enemy lines, we had been caught in the open. A shell erupted into the ground nearby – the spotting round. While the rest of our patrol sped off, my own vehicle refused to start. We sat there, our Land Rover's engine coughing weakly, almost like a kitten, knowing all the time that someone was watching us. As I and everyone else in our vehicle looked round to see where the shell had come from, that man was quietly feeding instructions to the soldier charged with aiming and firing the weapon. Next time, I knew, they wouldn't miss.

A jolt, probably turbulence, snaps me back into the present. As I woozily try to recover my focus, we're given the sign that I've been dreading since I clambered onto the plane: we've reached an altitude where we need to clamp our oxygen masks onto our faces. It's not as bad as breathing under water but my claustrophobia intensifies. There's something unnerving, almost inhuman, about hearing your breath coming in loud rasps. It reminds me of going to the dentist when I was a kid.

We have all switched on now. I can feel something beginning to sweep through my body. It is not fear, exactly. I have never entered a terrified, fight-or-flight state. If I did, then I'd be really worried, because it would mean that I was panicking. What I experience instead is a state of heightened focus.

3

Everyone is in their own headspace now. It's good, this nervous energy. You need it. I have always thought that this time must be similar to what footballers experience as they wait in the tunnel for a match to start. Hearing the roar of the crowd. Clearing their minds of everything except what they need for the next hour and a half. Everything for them, as it is for us, is about *right here* and *right now*. Nothing else matters.

A dim red light comes on above the plane's rear door. Two minutes to go. We stand and the loadmaster ushers us towards the rear of the plane. I look around at my mates' faces. None of us like this. We know we're not going to be jumping into clear skies. Tonight is a dusk jump. We're all anxious about the murk outside. Night jumps are the worst. There's so much kit, you're going so fast, that the risks of disaster increase exponentially. Everyone here is aware of the stories of the lads who didn't land safely. There have been deaths and injuries in the past. There will be deaths and injuries in the future. It's another of those uncomfortable ideas we've all had to get used to.

The danger of a collision is exacerbated at night, when the only way of spotting one of your comrades is the red glow stick on the front of one of their ankles, and the green one on the rear. It's like watching fireflies, or tracer. There are times jumping at night when there are so many darting streaks of colour in the sky that I struggle to believe that we are not drifting above a firing range.

The doors open. There is a powerful rush of fresh air. We waddle up towards the lip of the doorframe, struggling with the cumbersome weight of the ammunition, radios, food, water and all the other operational equipment we're carrying.

As I approach the door, I'm suddenly enveloped by the shocking cold of the atmosphere outside. The green light comes on. This is it. Away we go.

Except, there is nothing dramatic about our exit from the plane. The idea is that you don't leap, you ease yourself out, as if you're sitting down in an armchair. Somebody who jumps like a kid splashing into a swimming pool will be spun round by the wind. But if you get it right, it's like whooshing down a big slide.

As soon as I let go, I feel the slipstream grabbing hold of my body. The sheer force of it pushes me sideways before I begin my descent. My canopy won't unfurl in its entirety for another couple of hundred feet. For the moment I'm still dropping, dropping, dropping, dropping. I shout, 'One thousand.' My guts have leaped into the roof of my mouth. None of my organs seem to be able to adjust to the pace at which I am travelling. 'Two thousand.' My heart, my liver, my lungs; they all appear to be in a different place from the rest of my body. 'Three thousand.'

I ready myself for the colossal thump of the canopy once it's filled with air, then the jolt forward as my entire momentum is altered. For a second, I will be lifted *upwards*, like a puppet being jerked on a string, then the drift down can begin.

I'm always relieved once that moment has been negotiated safely. From that point on, I should be able to control my descent. When you get it right, even though you are still hurtling through the sky at an unbelievable pace, it seems as if you're floating slowly and elegantly down.

When you're so high, surrounded by the frigid ozone, your comrades below descending in elegant S-shapes, you feel like a spaceman. You have the astronaut's sense of giddy wonder at the perspective you have been granted on the world beneath you. It's only when other men shoot past you, or the wind turns and you look at your GPS, that you can comprehend the lethal speed at which you're travelling.

You think to yourself: *This is special.*

At least, that's what should happen. Because this evening something has gone wrong. My exit from the plane wasn't clean. Instead of easing myself gracefully into clear air, I realise I must have wobbled into the sky. Now I can see the cords of my parachute are tangled. The wind and the weight of my gear send me tumbling round and round.

The constant, nauseous twisting dislodges my goggles. Suddenly my eyes feel assaulted by a fierce, unrelenting rush of wind. Worse, I can feel my oxygen mask slipping until it is half off. *Fuck, this is* not *good. There is* nothing *good about this.* As the flow into my lungs slackens I start to feel dizzy. I cannot afford to pass out, and at this height I won't have long before my body and mind begin to shut down. My cold fingers scrabble around the edge of my mask, trying and eventually managing to make it cover my mouth.

But I am still plummeting through the atmosphere, if I can't properly open the chute soon it'll be too late. Adrenaline is sluicing through my body. My mind is frantic.

I need to work out what I can do to save myself. I don't do these jumps that often, I don't have the stored-up reserves of experiences that mean I can contemplate what is happening to me calmly. But I know I cannot spiral into a blind panic. You've got to try to find that still point, otherwise it's so easy to make things worse.

Should I try to get myself out of this twist, or would it be better to just release my main chute and open the reserve? Even if I manage to resolve the tangle it might not be enough to save the situation, because there are always new problems you've not anticipated. But if I discard my first parachute and pull the reserve handle, that means another freefall, and no guarantee I'll have any more luck. *OK*, I think, taking deep draughts of oxygen to try to steady my racing heart. *I can fix this.*

I start kicking to loosen the twisted cords. Each attempt sends me spinning back in the opposite direction, which in turn threatens to tangle me further. Eventually I manage to work myself free and instantly the canopy opens and my descent loses the jerky, uncertain quality that had been so alarming. I take a moment to compose myself, then attempt to locate the other lads in my stick.

I begin to start fiddling with my GPS, but it is twenty degrees below zero and without mittens my fingers feel numb, swollen and clumsy; it's almost impossible to make the device function. It's at just this moment that I pass through a large cloud. Instantly my world shrinks to the dense fog that envelops me. My eyes, unprotected by goggles, are scratched at by sleet and hail. To top it all my radio ear-piece has tumbled out.

Everything that could have gone wrong so far, has gone wrong. I catch myself wondering: *What the fuck is going to happen next?*

When I emerge into clear sky I feel a moment's relief. This is followed by more anxiety. With only a couple of thousand feet to go, I've still no idea where the rest of the stick is. All I do know is that I'm miles away from the drop zone. I'd expected to see it – a tidy green space suitable for landing – somewhere beneath; instead, there is a small village. The loadmasters must have dropped us off at the wrong location.

A little distance away is a small field. It's not where I'm supposed to be landing, but it looks safe and free from obstacles. I turn my parachute towards it. As I drift closer, I notice that it's bisected by a muddy brown track. This in itself is not a problem. What is a threat is the row of telegraph poles that stand either side of the path. *Shit*, I think, *if I hit them, then that's it for me.*

I tug hard on the cords, hooking my parachute around so that I'm facing in the opposite direction. But though I've managed to avoid crashing into the telegraph poles, the wind is now behind me. You're not supposed to land like that, because you want to be slowing down as you approach the ground. The gust at my back is forcing me to accelerate over the last few feet. The ground seems to be hurtling up *towards* me. I crash into it and my world becomes a jumbled mess. I turn over and over and see the grey of sky, then the green of the grass. The grey of sky, then the green of the grass. The grey of sky, then the green of the grass.

Eventually my momentum slows and I come to a crumpled stop. Breathless, my body a symphony of pain, I lie there for a few seconds, gingerly moving each of my limbs to see if any bones have been crushed in the fall. My head is spinning, everything pulses with agony, but it seems I am OK.

I need to find my mates, because we have work to do. *Right*, I tell myself, a mixture of excitement and relief – almost elation – singing in my blood, *let's get started*.

✷

Here's the thing about the people that end up in the SAS. Most of them are like me: normal, jeans-and-T-shirt-wearing kinds of blokes from council estates. We're not supermen, we're not James Bonds or ninjas, we don't have magic powers. We're not special, there's no mystery about us and there's no room for bullshitters, or people with airs and graces: we're just resilient, dedicated soldiers.

But I have led a life that has exposed me to an extraordinary range of experiences and I'm excited to tell you my story. I'm proud of the journey that has taken me from being a terrified boy chased home from school by racist bullies to a soldier in first the army, and then the SAS, where I was one of the first British-born Black men to join the regiment. I've served everywhere from Northern Ireland to the Middle East, as well as a whole host of places I can't tell you about, protecting the country I love so much. In the years since I retired from the forces, I've travelled to some of the world's most dangerous places to help protect charity workers and journalists as they do their incredible work in the aftermath of natural disasters, or in brutal conflict zones.

There have been mad times, bad times, sad times and crazy times. I've had emotional, physical and psychological trauma; financial struggles and health problems; I've been through grief and divorce; I've lost close mates and close family members; and I've experienced bullying and racial harassment. It's been a lot, though maybe not much more than most people encounter. What I believe, however, is that you can get through it all if you've got the right willpower, the right mindset.

I wasn't born fearless, or strong, or confident. Those things are the result of hard work and a willingness to learn from my mistakes, as well as a constant desire to push myself out of my comfort zone. The SAS's founder, David Stirling, laid down five principles that he wanted new recruits to his unit to live by: humility, integrity, humour, a classlessness and the unrelenting pursuit of excellence. I didn't set out deliberately to embody them, but I realise now that they have informed everything I've ever done.

There is no witchcraft in any of this. You don't need to be an elite soldier to follow Stirling's ideas. They might involve graft and dedication (nothing good ever comes easy), but they are simple and clear, and I believe can help you get the best out of yourselves, to live without limits, and to build the resilience you need to keep going when life throws one of its curveballs (which it will).

This book won't shy away from the darkness and challenges we all encounter. At the same time, I also want it to carry a positive message, because that's the sort of person I am. No matter how tough things get, I'm always convinced that I *will* get out the other side. Some things will hit you harder than others. You might need to take one step back to take two steps forward. But as long as you're still breathing, you're still in the game. More than that, I believe that we're on this planet to live life and enjoy it. I don't take things for granted, and never have done. And so I thrive on everything.

I hope I can help you do the same.

1
NEVER BACK DOWN

Everyone loved Sam Downes. Especially women. Sammy, as people outside our family knew him, took such pride in the way he presented himself to the world. His manners were perfect. He'd always be suited and booted, even if he was just out for a couple of pints. Shoes polished, tie and white shirt immaculate. The smell of Old Spice. He wasn't bothered that the other men in the pubs he went to had black around their eyes from the pits, or hadn't shaved. At Christmas he'd put on a dinner jacket, the only one at his working men's club who did. He just wanted to show that he cared.

Sam, my dad, was part of the Windrush generation. He was 18 when he left Clarendon in Jamaica. Like so many of the people that made that journey, he was a patriot – the sort that would have a picture of the Queen on their wall – who thought he was coming to the motherland. He expected to be welcomed with open arms. But, of course, it wasn't like that. He arrived in a country where people were still putting up 'No blacks, no Irish, no dogs' signs. Later, he'd tell me about seeing them as he wandered, with Irish friends, trying to find a boarding house that would give them a room.

There was a part of him that was always on guard. Whenever he was in a pub, even one he'd been going to for years, he'd stand with his back to the wall. I think sometimes: *What must he have been through before I was born that taught him to be so wary? How many mistakes did he make before he learned?*

And yet he also believed that you should be free to go wherever you wanted. He'd walk into anywhere. Talk to anyone. That's the sort of person he was. Nothing was out of bounds for him. And the thing about Sammy was, he seemed to change other people. He didn't argue with them or try to make them feel bad about stuff they said or thought. He just showed them that he was someone who deserved respect.

Some of that was because of the way he carried himself and treated others. And some of it was because he stood up for himself. He wasn't a bully and he never went out looking for a fight, but he had a reputation for always standing his ground. If he saw another person having a tough time he'd want to help. He couldn't bear the idea of being somebody who just walked by. I remember the first time I witnessed this side of him. I was outside a pub near our home, nursing a bottle of pop and a packet of crisps while Dad drank inside. A man started on a woman; I didn't know why. Then, suddenly, my dad had emerged from the pub and was right by them, shouting, 'Hey, pack it in!' in his broad West Indian accent.

In response, the man started abusing him. The same vicious, racist stuff Dad must have heard so many times before. But he wasn't prepared for how this small, balding but dapper figure tore into him. One punch after another, then a headbutt, going at the man like a little hurricane. I was terrified; there's nothing that can prepare a kid for a sight like that. And then, a few seconds later, Dad was back outside the pub, talking to me, as if he'd just gone to get a pack of fags from the shop. The only signs of anything unusual were the deep-red blood stains on his shirt.

We never talked about why he was like that. But, looking back, it's obvious: he *needed* to be. If he hadn't, he wouldn't have survived for a minute.

□

I don't know how he ended up in a small place like Stoke. There wasn't any sort of West Indian community to speak of in this poor, white working-class town in the North Midlands. But there was work. Dad was a manual labourer. Pits, then building sites, then the pottery factories we called potbanks: graft that left his body scarred but strong. He wasn't a big man, but he was hard as nails, with hands as tough as a rhino's hide. Right through his life he'd walk for miles to work, whatever the weather, in his overalls. Even later, when he was at a factory, people would see him running up and down flights of stairs on his breaks.

My mum, June, was 16 when she met Sammy, in 1957. When she was 17, her own mum kicked her out. Dad had the wrong colour skin – my grandmother was one of the few human beings whose mind he couldn't change.

The young couple didn't have much money, so they started their lives together in bedsits, living alongside other recent immigrants in parts of Stoke called Shelton and Cobridge. My brother Stephen was born first, in 1959. Then, five years later, I came along.

I spent the first three and a half years of my life surrounded by people who had come to Britain from all over the world.

I remember men in turbans, women in brightly coloured dresses, and the smells that came from different cuisines being prepared at the same time. It always surprises people how much I can recall from those times. It surprises *me*, to be honest. It comes to me a bit like a dream. There was Jean, a big plump woman in a green velvet dress who used to look after me. Jean was the landlady of the big house we lived in. I have this memory of her holding me on a balcony. Another image is me standing up in my pushchair, looking over the railings onto the canal below, accompanied by two young Indian men who used to take me for walks.

When I was almost four we moved from our bedsit to a flat of our own in a council estate called Bentilee, which when it was built ten years before had been the largest bit of social housing in Europe. It was only four miles away, and yet it was like landing on another planet. The first place we lived was a two-bedroom flat on Kendal Grove, which somehow managed to feel roomy after the bedsit.

The people of Bentilee were overwhelmingly white. Most of them had jobs in the mines or local factories. Back then, Stoke wasn't just a potbank renowned for its pottery, it also had several pits. Everybody in the city seemed to work with their hands. And everyone seemed to work hard.

The streets were full of smog, from the factories that belched fumes day and night. There was no relief indoors, either, because everyone constantly smoked cigarettes: in offices, houses, working men's clubs and buses. There were nights when the fog in my dad's club was so thick that I couldn't find him. That's what we smelled right through my childhood: fags, smoke from the factories and oatcakes, the local speciality.

Although it was the sixties, there were parts of Stoke that might as well have been Victorian. You'd still see rag-and-bone men, blokes in heavy leather jackets and flat caps delivering coal from a cart, and housewives in headscarves. But what I almost never saw was people like me. There were 4,500 homes on the estate. Only one of them was occupied by another Black family.

¤

Overnight we were confronted by something that was new to my brother and me, but probably painfully familiar to my parents. Some of our new neighbours didn't want us living near them. They appeared to hate us and didn't care if we knew.

Men and women spat at us, and called us niggers. They hurled abuse from the tops of buses, or as they cycled past us, or as they crossed our paths on the pavement. We never responded. We'd just keep walking in the same direction. The only sign my mum or dad would give that something unusual was happening would be the way they squeezed my hand more tightly. Sometimes I'd ask questions: 'Why are they saying that, Dad?' or 'Why don't you do anything?' Dad would just say, 'Ignore them, ignore them.' He got more abuse than any of us, but I think my mum – who had filth like 'nigger lover' screamed at her – suffered most. It left me angry, hurt and perplexed. It wasn't clear to me why we were being singled out in this way.

On my first day at school, I turned up wearing a beautiful cardigan my mum had knitted. It was yellow with two brown bunnies. I'll never forget it, nor how proud I was when I put it on. That morning, we were all assigned lockers where we could store our PE kit and everything else we needed for the day, and above each locker was a little symbol that was supposed to help us recognise it as ours. One boy had a soldier, I was sick with jealousy about that. Another had a football. The girls had things like rainbows, teddy bears and dollies. Then it was my turn. 'Here you are, Melvyn, this is yours,' said the teacher, smiling. I got a gollywog. The thing is, I don't believe she wanted to hurt or humiliate me. I think she thought it would help. But you don't realise, unless you wear the skin, how awkward, how bad these experiences can make you feel.

This sort of thing happened a lot. At story time, the teacher might read a book called *Little Black Sambo*, which was about a young kid who had adventures with tigers. Again, there was no malice in her choice. Still, it ensured that among my classmates, my name became 'Sambo'.

For a while I didn't fully make the connection between words like Sambo and the colour of my skin. Then, one day, a Black guy walked past the school and all the kids streamed over to the gate, shouting 'Black sambo'. Almost without thinking I started doing the same. At this, a boy turned to me and said, 'No, you're a Black sambo too. Look at you, you're Black.' He began to rub my skin – to get the black off, he said. I followed his lead. When I thought about it later, I realised that something about me really was different.

◻

When we moved to Bentilee we bought our first telly, an enormous black and white one. The person we saw on it that really inspired me and Stephen was Muhammad Ali. It wasn't just his charisma or his skill: he looked like me. This meant a lot.

Everybody at school knew Muhammad Ali. They'd pretend to fight like him in the playground: all these kids running round shouting, 'Float like a butterfly, sting like a bee.' And he made us so proud. He enlarged our sense of what was possible.

The telly might have been where we saw Muhammad Ali, but it was also full of stuff that affected me in other ways. This was the time of the Black and White Minstrels. There were shows like *Love Thy Neighbour*, *Rising Damp* and *Till Death Us Do Part*, where people would talk about 'wogs' and 'coons' accompanied by a laughter track. Almost any time a Black person who wasn't also a legendary athlete came on television they were degraded, or shown doing stupid things. In a lot of these shows the joke was supposed to be on the person who was abusing Black people – my dad always laughed when he watched them – but not everybody saw that side. All they heard were those words. The next day, in the playground, they'd be shouting them at me.

□

There was a mile's walk between our flat and my school. Over the course of my life, I have been a scared teenage recruit hiding just metres away from an IRA enforcer, I have seen comrades torn limb from limb before me, I've dodged car bombs and bullets in the chaos of post-invasion Baghdad, I've been in earthquakes and flooded cities, I have looked death in the face more times than I can count. Nothing has been as terrifying as that journey.

Some days, Mum or Dad would be able to drop me off or pick me up because they were off work, or on night shifts. I liked those days because I felt safe, although we still had to pretend not to hear all the abuse that was hurled at us. On other days, Stephen, who was at the senior school by then, could accompany me part of the way. But that didn't make much of a difference either. He and I were walking back from the oatcake shop one time when a group of grown men looked up from the digging they were doing and shouted, 'What you little coons want?' Then they started to call us 'niggers' and other names. We walked faster, trying not to show our fear but also desperate to get away as soon as we could. They carried on, 'What are you looking at?' then ran at us, brandishing their shovels. As soon as we kicked into a sprint, they started laughing.

Mostly, however, I was alone. I hated it. There are times now when my cat gets spooked and you can see the nerves flickering through his body. Every tiny movement or noise fills him with terror. That was me then. It was like being a hunted animal.

Getting to school, going through the gates: that was fine. But during the lunch break I'd get a first taste of the trouble waiting for me. Some of the older boys would threaten me: 'You're going to get a proper kicking today.' They were hard kids – four years older than me, far taller, more sure of their strength than I was; the estate had sharpened their aggression to a savage point. I knew they'd be waiting for me later on. And *they* knew that once I was out on the streets, I'd be vulnerable, a tiny boy with nobody to protect him.

The fear would mount as the end of school approached. I'd be gripped by nervous tension, and start trying to work out which route home would be safest for me that day. Do I go out of the front gate? Do I leave by the rear entrance? Do I cross the concrete football pitches and climb a set of six-foot railings that were twice my height? I'd never do the same route two days in a row. I didn't want them to be able to predict where I'd come out. Sometimes, though, the bullies would find me before I'd had a chance to decide. Panic-stricken, I'd push my way past other kids, heedless of them or teachers shouting at me, and rush to the door, ignoring whatever I'd left in my locker. I'd scramble over the railings – twice, I almost impaled myself on them – and onto the main road below, so terrified that I'd barely even glance at the pavement I was tumbling onto.

I'd crash onto the rough tarmac, hard enough that for a second all the wind would be knocked out of my lungs, then I'd sprint, my body flooded with adrenaline, my heart thudding in my chest, a howling, spitting gang of kids on my heels – shouting racist abuse, leering as they told me what they'd do if I fell into their clutches. Sometimes I'd catch a glimpse of my reflection as I hurtled past one of the street's highly polished windows: a slight boy in hand-me-down clothes, small even for my age, with a head haloed by an Afro and a face distorted by terror. I'd bang on the doors of any house I could reach, hoping that somebody would open the door and save me.

If I was lucky an old lady in a scarf might come out, yelling: 'Go away, leave him alone. Leave him be.' They'd usually be sympathetic, patting me on the head and asking me where I was from and if I liked it in this country. I'd always think, *But I'm from here*. That was something I'd grown used to. Even when

I'd go to the shops with my mum, women would say, 'Oh, isn't he lovely, can I touch his hair?' as if I was a dog.

Now I realise that the terror I felt at being chased was out of all proportion to the actual physical threat. On the days when the bullies did manage to catch me, they'd usually just play around with me, flicking me, pushing me onto the ground, making monkey noises. It was humiliating more than anything else. And yet in the middle of the atmosphere they had created, it felt as if they wanted to kill me. It meant that there were times when I wanted more than anything to be white, because surely then, I thought, they'd leave me alone.

Every day was like a recurring nightmare, one that I couldn't wake from no matter how hard I tried. It felt as if it would never stop, that things would never get better. But then, one day, they did. I was seven by this stage; the bullying had been going on for more than a year. That afternoon, I'd been pursued almost the whole way home when I spotted my dad.

He had recently moved pits and was working nights, so we saw a bit more of him. He was smoking outside the house during a break in play from the cricket he'd been watching on television. He loved seeing those great West Indian teams – he'd go without sleep to do it.

As soon as I caught sight of him, I thought, *I'm saved.* I hadn't told my parents, or my brother, what I was going through. Here, though, I saw my chance to change that. When I was 70 metres away from home I started screaming, 'Dad, Dad, Dad!'

The pack behind me stopped and watched as I crossed the road to tell him what was going on. I launched into my story

24

immediately, words tumbling messily out of my mouth as I tried to explain. 'They're always fighting me.' He listened, then spoke immediately. 'Right, go fight them.' We'd never talked about fighting before; he'd never shown me how to throw a punch or anything like that. But I could tell he was serious. 'Fight them. Don't back down.' I felt bewildered. Fear still rocketed through my veins but now I was confused too. 'I can't fight them, Dad. There's more of them.'

'Fight them. Bite them if you have to.' I was still reeling from this. 'No. *No*. Dad.' He remained unmoved. 'If you don't fight them,' and now he made as if to remove his belt, 'you're going to get this.' Dad was a disciplinarian from the West Indian school. I didn't want to be hit. I was also anxious – in a way I did not fully understand – not to disappoint him.

So that was that. I crossed the road towards this group of kids, who were still trying to work out what we'd said to each other. I took a few steps then stopped and stared back at my dad. He just stood there. To begin with, the bullies appeared shocked by what I was doing. Then, as I got closer, they ran towards me, ready to start their kicking and punching. Blows rained in on me. It was hot and close. Limbs flailed everywhere. At that point I grabbed an arm and sank my jaws right into it. I tasted flesh, sweat, the cotton of his shirt, and felt my teeth hit bone. There was an outraged squeal and the assault on me slackened as my attackers tried to process what had happened. I could also sense, from the edge of my vision, that my dad was finally coming over. They all waited for one second, then two, then ran.

▢

Later that night he sat me down and started talking to me. We didn't do this sort of thing very often. He was a man of his time. He wasn't the sort who'd take us to the cinema; he wasn't a touchy-feely person; he never told me he loved me, except when he'd had a drink. I looked into his eyes and could see how much it had hurt him to send me back across the road like that. He wasn't a violent man, and this was nothing to be celebrated, just a horrible thing that had to be done. But there was a smile on his lips that told me he was proud. I'll never forget that. 'Always look after yourself,' he said, 'never back down. Because if you back down once, you'll always back out, no matter what. Leave a mark. Bite them, kick them, get your fingers in their eyes, do whatever you need to do. But don't back down.'

The next day something changed. The abuse didn't stop. And yet at the same time I could tell that the kids had become wary of me. I have to think that those who bullied me didn't know better. Nobody's born a racist. However, if you've seen your dad spit at or abuse a Black family, you're going to think that sort of behaviour is OK. More than that, they were just kids being kids. Sometimes that involves being cruel in ways that adults don't understand.

I'd changed too. I was more confident. I started having fights. I didn't start them, but if one came I'd always fight back. Before you knew it, I had a reputation. Best fighter in my year, best fighter in my school. That carried on into senior school. I still don't really know how it ever got arranged, but there'd be these massive duels between the best fighters from each of the different schools on the estate. Luckily, this was before kids started carrying knives.

I never went looking for a scrap, but I always had that thought from my dad in my head: never back down. Once that's in you, it's difficult to shake off.

¤

Bentilee had a reputation as the worst estate in Stoke-on-Trent. When I got older I learned that you should never mention you came from there when you were trying to chat up girls or they'd run a mile.

It was rough. The kids were scruffy. It was run-down, even though it was only a few years old. There was crime and lots of fighting, outside pubs, schools.

But most men and women there were like my parents, working their fingers to the bone. Just like now, there was only ever a minority who skived, or were druggies, or who tossed their rubbish onto the street. The rest of us were proud: we looked after our gardens, we loved living there.

Not long after I'd stood up to the bullies, we moved to another home on the estate, closer to my school. My parents were ecstatic; it was a three-bedroom semi-detached house in red brick with a toilet upstairs.

Our new neighbours were less pleased. They tried to start a petition to stop us from moving in. Twice we had our windows put through, once while we were sitting in the room. The first Christmas Eve after we'd moved in, our house was burgled. We'd spent the day at my auntie's before coming back home. Everything had been trashed. The Christmas tree was knocked over, surrounded by a fringe of smashed decorations. The walls had been covered with writing, 'Niggers fuck off, from the Phantom

Turkey Fuckers', and swastikas. My brother and I were upset, but my parents took it even harder. From that night on, for months afterwards, my dad slept downstairs on the settee with a huge kitchen knife beside him. He was sure that they'd try again. 'I'll kill them. I'll kill them,' he said, which shook me. It wasn't what had happened so much as what it had done to my dad. That knife, sitting in the lounge, was a sign that we couldn't feel safe in our own home.

Not everyone was like that. The family on the other side, Mr and Mrs Edwards, were brilliant. They were beautiful people. She'd make us cakes. And I'd help Mr Edwards in his garden. He'd give me sixpence in return, but the thing I was really there for were his stories from the war, where he'd been a Desert Rat. He called the Arabs 'wogs', because he didn't know better. But the thing he really got worked up by were the flies. 'They were everywhere,' he'd tell me. 'You could be miles from the nearest settlement, but there they'd be, covering your food.' All I could think was, *Why is he so bothered about flies?*

Years later, when I came back from the First Gulf War, the street put a little party on to welcome me home. I was a married man of 26 by this stage. As soon as he saw me, Mr Edwards ran over and shook my hand. The first thing he said was, 'The flies. The flies.' And he was totally right: 50 years of technological progress had done absolutely nothing to stop flies from crawling all over your fresh rations.

'Those flies,' I said to him, laughing, 'I *hated* those flies.'

¤

Time went by. We built a reputation. We showed everyone around us what sort of people we were. It didn't happen overnight, but a moment came when we realised that our family was loved.

This was important, because life for us, as for almost all our neighbours, was tough. There was lots of laughing and joking in our house, but my family was also the kind where if the washing machine broke it would be a crisis. Everything was on tick. Hard as my parents worked, and although there was always good food on the table, we didn't really have a bean to put together. In our first flat, we had a piss bucket under our bed, which we'd empty each morning. We shared bathwater (I'd be the last in the tub, scrubbing myself in what was now a grey-looking slop) and wore hand-me-down clothes. Some weeks we wouldn't have the money to pay the rent so we'd hide when the rent collector came to our street. As soon as he'd gone, the lights would go back on, but we never let too many payments go by unpaid – my parents had a fear of being in debt.

On top of that, there was what my mum was going through.

Through a lot of my childhood, Mum worked in a cake shop. If she was in an up mood she'd give me and my mates freebies. But on another day she could be frighteningly harsh, or bitter in the way she treated me and Stephen. My brother and I could never really follow her moods. We just didn't know what was wrong with her. She'd be happy one moment, dead moody the next. The wrong word at the wrong time and her slipper would be off and you'd get a belt round the head. This was most obvious when other kids came over. Then, when I got older, she'd alternate between being incredibly nice and incredibly spiteful to my girlfriends. It could appear at times like she was jealous of us.

That up and down never left her. She could turn nasty out of nowhere. I'd have a jug of coffee dumped on me without knowing what I'd said out of turn. That's not easy for an adult, but it's even more unsettling when you're a kid and you don't know what mood your mum is going to be in from one moment to the next.

It's so clear now that my mum had serious issues. She was just one of those people that found life harder. And if you think about the start she had, that's not a surprise.

There was a lot about her life that we didn't find out until years later, at her funeral. Her dad had died when she was young, in the war. Her mother remarried and had a couple more kids before her new husband died, then she married once more. I guess everybody handles grief in different ways. My grandmother dealt with it by picking on my mum. She'd decided that her eldest child was responsible for her first husband's death and couldn't forgive her for it. She made her sleep on cold floors – her sisters remember having to step over her when they got out of their beds. Sometimes they'd try to get her to join them under the covers to get warm. I just can't imagine what it must have been like for her.

After she had been thrown out, she kept in touch with her sisters, and eventually restored some sort of relationship with her mother. We only went a handful of times to my grandmother's – and never with my dad. I wasn't really aware of what had gone on before. I didn't know about the abuse or the fallout after my parents' marriage. But I wasn't stupid; I could sense how uninviting this environment that smelled of piss and mouldy biscuits was. You could feel my grandmother's bitterness and resentment.

Mum had a similar relationship with God. My grandmother had been religious, and Mum seemed to bounce back and forth with it. One moment she'd be trying to drag us along to church, the next her interest would fall off a cliff. It was as if she was grabbing for something to cling on to. I can see how lonely and abandoned she must have felt.

Nothing got easier for her. After I was born she had a couple of miscarriages. Then, in her early thirties, she had a hysterectomy. She was in and out of mental hospitals and shelters. There were a couple of suicide attempts – a response to all of the trauma she'd accumulated. How much did I understand? Not a lot. Nothing was ever really explained to us. The ambulance would pull up outside our house, take her away, and then we'd not see her again for another few weeks. Dad would carry on working and going out to the pub. Our aunties might pop round. Mostly, though, Stephen and I just looked after ourselves.

As if stuff couldn't get much worse for her, when I was eight she got cancer for the first time. My dad sat me and my brother down and tried to explain what was happening. But I didn't know what cancer was; it was another thing that didn't make sense. I just knew that something was deeply wrong. It was the only time I ever saw Dad cry. Still, she fought it off. Then it returned in another part of her body, so she fought it off again.

All of this affected my parents' marriage. They never stopped loving each other, but it could be tricky at times. My mum would often go mad at my dad. There'd be arguments, shouting. Dad wasn't a saint. Who is? Who *wants* to be? But other men might have left. He didn't. He took responsibility. He'd committed to that marriage.

Sometimes he'd try to take her out to their club to get her to enjoy herself. He'd be quiet until he'd got a few drinks down him and then somebody would ask, 'Give us a song, Sammy Downes.' God, he loved to dance and sing. He had a lovely voice and sang Nat King Cole, The Stylistics, people like that, beautifully. But Mum would inevitably end up falling out with someone there, or sit looking miserable, nursing a whisky in the corner.

Dad's glass was always half full. Mum's was always half empty. That's just the way they were. There was a lot of moaning, a lot of feeling down. On a couple of occasions, after an argument with Dad, she called us racist names. 'It's your fault, you two wogs.' I guess it was the pressure she felt she was under. And yet I know she loved us. She always did the best she could – I don't doubt that for a second. Like my dad, she was a real grafter; she emptied herself for us. The surprise isn't that she kept on breaking down; it was that she was able to go on at all.

¤

My parents were both resilient, they just showed it in different ways. Perhaps this was because they had different personalities, or maybe it was that they were facing different challenges.

Mum did complain, she did grouse, but she kept going and going. She went through cancer, severe depression and rejection by her own family, and she came out the other side. I don't know how she managed working full time with playing the role of a traditional wife, looking after us kids and making sure dinner was on the table when Dad came back from his shift. Several nights a week, while she was washing up, he'd get changed and go to the pub. I think she knew that sometimes survival is its own kind of victory.

Dad was more buoyant. His response to bad times wasn't to grit his teeth and hold on, like Mum did. He smiled. He was determined to enjoy music, drink, the company of other human beings. He knew that the world has its share of bad people, and he knew that life has its share of horrors and traps, but that didn't stop him being open and curious. It didn't stop him wanting to help anyone he thought was in need. Most of all, it didn't stop him being positive.

I've tried to take inspiration from them both. If I see someone getting abused or beaten up, I'll step in. I hate bullies. I remember how they made me feel, what it did to me. It knocks your self-esteem and confidence. It makes you feel less than human, like a second-class citizen.

The bullying I was subjected to, in fact all of the racism we encountered, was a horrible experience, and yet it also helped make me more resilient. I wouldn't be the person I am now without it. The thing that my dad understood then, and I didn't, was that it always feels better when you don't duck a challenge: when you do what you know is the right thing. Because until you stand up for yourself, nothing will ever change. If I hadn't taken the fight back to those kids, they'd have kept going and going and going until they crushed me. Instead, I emerged stronger. That's the thing about tough times: when you next run into trouble, whatever shape it comes in, you can take inspiration from knowing that you've beaten adversity before. Once you've shown yourself you can do something once, it's easier to believe you can do it over and over again.

Even today, I'm still always drawing on that little well of defiance and bravery I dug for myself that day. I never wanted to let myself feel that vulnerable or scared again. Don't get me wrong, in the years since I've had more than my share of kickings, I've had some brutally low moments, but I've never backed down.

Of course, you don't always need to raise your fists or your voice – sometimes that's the last thing the situation needs – just do enough to prove to yourself that you're not beaten. If you've lost out on a promotion, don't lash out, use that anger and frustration to drive you to do better next time an opportunity comes up. You should always be looking to turn negative feelings into positive energy. Because when you realise that this is possible, it's like being taught the secret of perpetual motion. Every setback, every cruel word, every bereavement, every unexpected obstacle, becomes something you can use. Not just as evidence that, like my mum, you can survive anything that life throws at you, but as fuel you can burn to help you go further and faster than you ever thought possible.

2

DO THE DOG

've only got one tattoo. Half a dozen dots in Indian ink on my upper arm. A gang of us did it in the back of class: six 12-year-olds who thought they were something special.

It's almost the only mark that the time I was supposed to be learning left on me. School never made much sense. When I was 11 I went to Willfield High, a cheaply assembled mass of concrete and red brick that somehow always seemed to smell of damp clothes drying on radiators. Behind it was an old quarry that we'd clamber into at breaktimes so we could chuck rocks at each other.

To be honest, it wasn't much calmer once we were safely inside for lessons. Everyone there was from the Bentilee estate; we were all as poor and rough around the edges as each other. There was no uniform because they knew that nobody could afford them, and few of us even had rucksacks – that was a privilege only the well-off kids enjoyed – which meant that on the days when it was PE we brought in our kit in plastic bags. The game was to try to rip another boy's bag, which would see its contents spilling out into the playground, without having the same done to you.

I feel sorry for the teachers who came onto rowdy and chaotic estates like ours, but none of them gave the impression of actually wanting to be there. They just seemed to be counting down the hours until they could go home at the end of the day. If you were quiet, they made out you were stupid. They caned the ones who were noisy and disruptive.

They'd try to teach the few who were interested; the rest of us they left to mess about at the back of the classroom. The only concession to the curriculum was the tatty old textbooks they tossed at us. It was like a big holding pen, keeping us there until we were old enough to leave.

A good number of the teachers were sadists. It was like they just couldn't wait to give you a beating. There's something wrong with anybody who thinks a kid who's been talking in class should be beaten so hard that they are left with bruises. But then that had been true even at infant school. A teacher there once stabbed me in the arm with a pen.

If they weren't beating you or ignoring your existence, the teachers would talk down to you, calling you an idiot, making sure you understood that you'd never amount to anything. One man, an obese RE teacher, who stood out even there for his cruelty, told me, with a straight face, that Africans were obsessed by tribes. He was the sort who had written you off before he'd ever met you; he had a way of demeaning everyone.

A mate and I got our revenge on him by shooting his classroom's windows up with an air rifle one weekend. He caught me the following Monday holding a telescopic scope and, quite correctly, accused me of being involved. I, also quite correctly, pointed out that he couldn't prove anything.

There were exceptions. Roy Godwin, the PE teacher, was an inspiration. Less because of what he taught us, and more because he was kind and interested: he treated us like human beings and seemed to value what we had to say. In his own time he'd take us to his rugby club to watch him play matches. When his team went on the piss afterwards, he'd let us have a shandy. It helped that games was the thing I excelled at. I captained the school at football and rugby and ran cross-country; I loved anything that was physical or competitive.

In the classroom I was a daydreamer. I spent most of my time thinking about the military, which had been my biggest passion since I was a toddler. I couldn't understand geology or mathematics. I could only be enthusiastic if something interested me. I loved history because now and again they'd talk about wars: you could have asked me *anything* about the tanks or military formations of the Second World War. I liked geography when it helped me place where battles had been fought, or army units were currently stationed; beyond that I struggled to focus.

What was important to me and my friends, apart from sport, was music. We were obsessed with songs and the clothes musicians wore. They were brilliant in themselves, but they also helped us work out who we were, and weren't. At some point in the late seventies we stopped scribbling our names on our desks and started trying to carve out pictures of The Specials, especially their logo with the black and white man in a trilby hat.

Like every kid then I listened to Slade, Thin Lizzy and The Sweet, but the thing that really took me was when ska came back to Britain, got mixed up with punk and came out the other side as 2 Tone. I loved the bands from that scene. Because it started in Coventry I got to see The Specials, Selector, Madness, Bad

Manners. Their songs were fun but inspirational. What really struck me, and super-charged their appeal, was that a couple of the groups had both Black and white members. That felt important – like they were showing a different side of England, one that me and my mates could identify with. A gang of us became rude boys. Suddenly people noticed us, because we'd started dressing smartly. We'd come into our school in our glittering tonic trousers, bright white socks and shiny black brogues, a Crombie coat draped over our shoulders. I remember one teacher looking at us, almost open-mouthed in astonishment. You could see he was thinking, *God, what's happened to you?*

If we couldn't see the bands play live, we'd go to youth clubs or discos that played their records. We also had a tiny cassette recorder we'd use to play their music over and over again as we spent endless evenings standing, bored but harmless, outside pubs we weren't allowed into and shops filled with things we couldn't afford. Even now, if I listen to 'Ghost Town', or 'Do the Dog', I'm instantly transported back to that time.

□

Outside school we were free. And when I think about that time of my life it all seems to be bathed in the glow from the long hot summer of 1976.

We'd spend all day in the fields that ran along the edges of the estate. Each time we left Bentilee it felt as if we were stepping into an adventure. Nobody stopped us from walking long distances away from our homes, and we'd roam the countryside, collecting birds' eggs – from swans, starlings and owls – which we stored in an upturned Subbuteo box filled with cotton wool to keep them safe. That was a big thing for us then, though it's hard to explain why now.

The only people who objected to what we were doing were the farmers whose fields we tramped across; the other big menace were cows, who often seemed to chase us. But I was a good kid really. A bit of mischief here and there, maybe, but not much more.

It was more that I was daring, always wanting to try new things, and not so bothered about how dangerous they were. We did what were called duffers: seeing how far you could jump across a nearby ravine, how high you could climb up into a tree. One mate of mine bet me that I couldn't jump off a two-storey building. If I managed it, he said, I could come to his for tea every day for a year. Almost without thinking I jumped, landing heavily. But this was worth the risk because they had real butter on their table, not margarine or dripping. And fair play, he kept to his side of the bargain. Though I don't know to this day how he explained to his mum why so much of his family's food was being eaten while she was out at work.

Some of what we did was pretty dumb. There was one lad, Manley, a Sabbath- and Zeppelin-obsessed rocker with long ginger hair who used to wear a cut-off denim jacket. I once fired an air rifle in his direction, aiming way over his head so I'd frighten him rather than actually hit him, or so I thought. The pellet looped up, then down, far faster and more steeply than I'd expected. It buried itself in his thigh. *Oops,* I thought, as he lumbered towards me, screaming in rage.

And then there was bonfire night. This was maybe the apex of all the chaos and wildness of those days. The idea was that you wanted to make the biggest bonfire on the estate, the most extravagant guy. In the lead-up to the day itself, we'd be collecting as much material to throw onto it as we could. We didn't care where it came from, or what it was made of, which meant that quite a few garages got raided for their asbestos roofing, which we'd break up and chuck onto the fire – as soon as they got hot enough the pieces exploded. Once the pyre was built, the priority was to protect it so that kids from the next green on couldn't burn yours down (we, of course, would try to do the same to them), so we'd end up sleeping on tatty mattresses beside a little campfire. It now seems insane that we went to such efforts to breathe in toxic fumes.

I had plenty of mates, but one person I didn't really hang out with was my brother. There were four and a half years between us. That's enough distance that you don't have that much in common. We scrapped a lot in the empty hours after we got home from school. I'd try to hit him, then run away and hide in the cold, damp little concrete toilet by the back door as he furiously banged on the wooden door. I knew I just had to stay there until 6.30, when Mum came back. We never talked about what we were going through, so we didn't even know that we'd both been bullied. For him, the racism was so bad that he decided to keep away. He barely went to school. When letters arrived at home telling my parents about his truancy he'd just rip them up and throw them away.

The other thing we didn't discuss was his name. He was always Stephen to me. He was Stephen all the way up to a couple of years ago when he asked us if we'd call him Delroy, which I'd

42

thought was his second name. He told us that on his first day at school a teacher had said, 'Delroy isn't an English name, we'll call you Stephen.' Even my parents called him Stephen. Looking back, I think maybe he had to find other ways of expressing the identity his teacher had tried to suppress. He grew dreadlocks, smoked marijuana with my dad and was deep into the music of Bob Marley.

But he's more of a home pigeon than I ever was. He's still on the same estate, working as a plumber. He could have gone to London, even abroad, and earned twice what he does in Stoke because he's so good at his job, but that wasn't for him. He only left the country for the first time when he was 42.

In that sense, he's a lot like loads of the lads I grew up around. Same routines, same pubs, same holidays. They've ended up doing what their dads did. Their kids will probably do the same.

I loved so much about growing up in Bentilee. It's the place that made me. I have millions of happy memories. I love going back, even now. But I'm glad that I had a way out.

□

I don't remember a time when I wasn't fascinated by soldiers. I'd be sitting in my pushchair, being hauled round one of the markets in Stoke, and I'd always want a little soldier with me. At first it was just seeing the uniforms, then everything deepened once I got to see them on TV. I was dazzled by watching the Trooping of the Colour on our old black and white screen. At some point it became an obsession. And if I hadn't made it into the army I'm sure I'd have been in the fire service, or become a police officer.

I'd always want to play at being soldiers with my friends. When I got home, I'd draw battle scenes, or painstakingly assemble and then paint Airfix kits. One of my biggest excitements was visiting the army careers office in the centre of Stoke. There'd always be an actual soldier there who would give me brochures that I'd take home, where I could paste pictures from it on my bedroom wall with a homemade glue made out of a mixture of flour and water.

This was a time when the culture was still saturated with the Second World War – it had come to an end less than a couple of decades after I'd been born. There were books and magazines and films about it – I'd never been a reader, but I devoured Sven Hassel's novels – and I grew up surrounded by men who had served in it. Some kept what had happened to them locked up inside them; others loved to talk about it. I'd pelt them with questions, desperate to know more.

There were a few guys that had memorabilia in their homes. One day, a neighbour called Mr Bolt gave me a real bayonet. A thrill went down my spine as I recognised it instantly. This was from the Wehrmacht! He wasn't even as close to being as excited about it as I was.

All of this meant that as soon as I heard about the existence of the army cadets I was desperate to go. I joined when I was 11. You didn't actually get a uniform until you were 13, but on the day that my mum took me up to Bucknall to sign up, the woman we spoke to said, 'Come down anyway.'

Every Tuesday I'd walk the two miles there and back in my own uniform of jeans and a Wrangler top, returning after ten o'clock, when it was already dark. Sometimes, if I was lucky, my mum would give me money for the bus. The couple that ran it, Staff Sergeant Banks and his wife, were, like my PE teacher Mr Godwin, an inspiration. They treated me like somebody who had a bright future. It was maybe the first thing, other than sport, I'd ever excelled at. I got all the badges and stars I could. I was given sergeant's stripes. Occasionally we'd go on annual camps with other local units, like the one from the slightly more cosmopolitan Cobridge, whose detachment had a couple of other Black faces. Though all of my friends were white and generally speaking I wasn't too bothered by spending most of my life as the only person of colour in any room I stepped into, sometimes it was nice to be reminded that there was a world beyond Bentilee.

Mostly, though, I was over the moon to be doing stuff that I thought was useful: first aid, camping, navigation, firing rifles. I'd already been keen on being a soldier; this hooked me. I didn't want anything to take me away from that path. It was my release from everything else that was going on in my life. I was 11 years old and they were letting me fire the Lee Enfield rifles that had been used in the Second World War. They were great beasts, nearly as big as me, with a recoil that knocked my slim frame backwards. I couldn't believe my luck. I got the same excitement and sense of purpose from everything we did in the cadets as the more academic kids must have got in lessons in school.

I'd show my friends what I'd learned – like building fires, how to make a bivouac from a bit of sheeting, or how to live off the land. Drawn in by my enthusiasm, some of them joined up, but very few stayed. They didn't like the discipline. This was at the same time as a lot of the kids my age starting getting into trouble: they ended up going to Borstal, or collecting criminal records.

Suddenly there were lads walking around with the money they'd got from robbing shops and houses. I never went down that route, though there were times when I felt tempted. I'd have a mate say, 'Can you come and keep watch? We'll pay you.' I could have done it. Chances are, I'd never have got caught. But I couldn't take that risk. First, I was worried my dad would kill me. Second, I was determined that I wouldn't do anything to jeopardise my plan to get into the army.

Just before I was old enough to get my uniform, a group of kids from a different area joined. They were older, 14 and 15. This was when *Roots* was on TV. I hated that programme. Not because of what it was about, but because, like the other shows of the time that had Black people in them, it offered all this material to bullies. These older lads would call me Kunta Kinte, one of the characters from it, or shout 'I'm going to whip you, *boy*!' in their best attempt at an accent from the Deep South. I hated it and nearly left. I wanted to fight them, and probably would have if I'd met them outside the cadets, but I didn't want to risk doing anything while I was actually in uniform that would give Sergeant Banks and his wife a reason to chuck me out. Luckily, like my mates before them, they couldn't stick the discipline and left after a few months.

The discipline was one of the things I loved. Not so much because I got a buzz from following orders, but because I recognised what it could do for me. You can either kick against discipline, or you can harness it to help you. Self-discipline is what helps you if you want to get up and go and do things. It makes you more of a worker and it gives you more resilience. It's what my self-confidence and can-do attitude spring from.

Like a lot of things, I reckon that comes from my dad. It was watching him and the way he went about his life that taught me about having the right values, about discipline.

Discipline was very important to him. That was the West Indian way. He didn't have many rules – don't ever bring the police round the house, look after Mum, use your manners and be a decent person – but we knew what would happen if we broke them.

I was that scared of being given the belt that even now I can remember the leather smell when he took it off. If we ever forgot our pleases or thank yous, or gave our mum some lip, he'd be on us in seconds. He wasn't scary as a person, but I really respected that discipline. I didn't want to let him down. He told us that if we showed other people respect, had good manners and tried to be decent human beings, we'd lead happy lives. Those principles have stayed with me.

And I owe my passion for fitness to him. He never set foot in a gym and he liked a drink, but by God was he fit. On Sunday afternoons, during that gap in the day when the pubs were shut, he'd come back tipsy, and carefully take his suit jacket and waist-coat off so that he was just in his shirtsleeves. He might give us sixpence if we could do 25 press-ups, or he'd encourage us to sit on his back while he did some press-ups himself. There was a lot of play-fighting; I'd hit him as hard as I could and he'd crumple to the floor, pretending I'd knocked him out.

I remember the feel of his muscles and his hands, which were tough as leather. He wasn't tall, or stocky, or anything like that, but he was so *strong*. I'd never have dared square up to him. Ever.

All the time, he would say, 'Box me, fight me.'

He loved it, I did too, and it's something I've taken with me through my whole life.

It's what still gets me up every morning to do some training before I've had anything to drink or eat, no matter what. If I don't do something on any given day, then something's gone wrong. I'll be grumpy; I'll have itchy feet; I stop being a nice person to spend time with. It's not about getting big, it's just part of being human.

Even if you're just walking in the fresh air, you're going to feel inspired. If I know it's going to rain the next morning, I'll *tell* myself that I'm going to go for a 10k jog, no excuses. Like my dad, I like a drink. Probably a bit too much: I can't just have one or two. But that means that the morning after I make sure I'm up early for a run. If I'm stuck in a hotel without a gym I'll run up and down the fire-escape stairs to get a sweat on. Because I know I'll feel better afterwards. It fixes my mental and physical states. It clears my head and ensures I'm in the right frame of mind to deal with whatever might come my way that day.

When I think back, I wonder whether my dad encourag-ing me to share in his love of fitness was his way of getting me started, getting me ready for life. It was a gift, really – something that had helped him navigate a world that wasn't always kind, or easy, or friendly. If you're going to face challenges, you want to be as physically and mentally fit as you can be. You need self-discipline.

It's not like he had a philosophy or anything like that, but he understood that small bits of discipline can give you the foundation to build something big. I find it easier to motivate myself because I've had the same routine, more or less, since I was 16.

If every morning you make sure you're neat and tidy, that your teeth are clean, then everything that follows is a bit easier. It sets your mindset for the day. We had that in the military, too. We had to make sure everything was clean: your body, your equipment, your bedding. If we knew we had an inspection the following day, we sometimes wouldn't even sleep in our beds, because we didn't want to disturb the perfect order we'd got them into.

Our beds weren't made up normally. Every single morning we made what were called bed blocks. We'd strip everything off the mattress, then the blanket had to be folded into a perfect square. Then the sheet would be folded into another square that matched the folded blanket's dimensions. Every part of your bedding had to be folded the same size – you'd end up with a perfectly symmetrical box: the bed block.

If you wanted to get it perfect, it meant getting up a couple of hours early, at least to begin with, when you were still getting used to it. After a while you got good at making bed blocks, so what had taken you two hours before could be completed in 30 minutes. The same principles were applied to everything.

The cupboards where we stored our uniforms and the rest of our kit had to be arranged immaculately. There was a particular way that the floors had to be polished (I can still remember the strange gluey smell of the wax we used). There was a right, and a wrong, way to shave.

This could all feel harsh, but it wasn't cruel, or pointless. It was all done for a reason. They wanted us to absorb these habits into our bloodstream so that we'd carry them over when we progressed to more complex things like learning tactics, or operating in the field. Our weapons had to be perfectly clean, inside and out. We had to put the bullets into our magazines in the correct way. Our medical kits had to be kept hygienic and organised.

If you have the basics right, then everything else follows. That's why the British Army is the best in the world, in my opinion. That's why the SAS was the best of the best. We check and we double-check until we're sure everything is right. Getting the basics right means your rifle doesn't suddenly misfire because there's sand in its mechanism. It means that your medical kit is up to date and stored in a place you can reach quickly. It means that you don't forget your map, or go out on a mission with a compass that doesn't work because it's got a bubble in it.

That discipline can feel tough, but ultimately it frees you, because it means you're liberated to do everything else without the nagging worry that you'll press your trigger and your weapon won't fire, or that you won't be able to find morphine if your mate gets hit.

I loved that way of thinking. And I try to take that mindset with me wherever I go. When you apply yourself, when you work hard on getting the basics right, then you build momentum. If you can show yourself that you can excel at small things, then you can start to believe that you might be able to achieve big things too.

Without it, I think it's possible I might never have left Bentilee, because it's a difficult place to break free of.

◻

I was the only one of my mates from school that followed the path I did. A lot of the rest of them went down the pits. Occasionally, in the early years of my time in the army, I envied them. They had a job that earned them respect in our community; they always had plenty of money in their pockets. I'd come back from leave and see them in the streets after their night shifts, their eyes still ringed with black dust. They'd have a quick shower, then be out at the pub. I remember thinking it was a brilliant way of life. But I also thought, *They're just like their dads.* That wasn't a criticism, it's just how it was.

And yet in the end their lives weren't the same as their fathers'. As the eighties drew on, their whole existence sort of collapsed. The pits were shut down and they had to find new work, in construction, or working on the roads. OK jobs, but never enough to replace what they had lost.

I was different. As soon as I left Bentilee I never looked back. That doesn't mean I had stopped thinking it was special; Stoke, Bentilee, has always been a haven for me. A refuge where I can go away from everything, and surround myself with people I've known my whole life. It was more that I knew that the world contained so much and I was desperate to see it. A little bit of adventurousness can go a long way.

51

Two weeks after I'd left school, I joined the army. I didn't have a single qualification to my name but I didn't care. The fat RE teacher whose windows I'd shot up had told me that I'd never make it in the army; I knew I was about to prove him wrong.

3

WHY ARE YOU HERE, SOLDIER BOY?

There's a picture of me aged 16, at the end of the year I spent as part of the Infantry Junior Leaders Battalion, my initial step into the British Army. My eyes are shaded by the brilliantly polished peak of my cap but you can see my smile, a smile that tells you everything you need to know about how proud and happy I am to be wearing this uniform. I look like there's nowhere else in the world I'd rather be. Which, as it happens, was absolutely true.

As soon as I joined my first unit – the Staffordshire Regiment – I started thriving. I just wanted to be a winner at everything. People used to tell me: 'You're green through and through,' which was really another way of saying that if you cut me, I'd bleed military. I loved everything about it. I loved the skills I was taught, the way that we were challenged both physically and mentally. Some people hated going out into the field on exercise, especially when it was cold and wet. Not me. The colder and wetter the better. As soon as one exercise had finished, I couldn't wait for the next to begin. And it might sound odd to anyone who grew up in a different kind of household, but God almighty I loved getting three proper hot meals a day. I'd been used to bits of toast spread with dripping. Here there was sausage and bacon and eggs and as much cereal as you could eat for breakfast. We might have pizza and chips for lunch and then a full roast in the evening. It blew my mind.

I spent the opening 12 months of my time in the army stationed in Gibraltar. It was exciting because it was new, but it was largely uneventful. We knew that Northern Ireland, where we were heading after short stints in Colchester and Germany, would be different.

◻

I wasn't scared about going, I was excited. At 19 years old, I was finally about to get the chance to do some proper soldiering. As proud as I'd been to guard the governor's mansion in Gibraltar, that wasn't really what I'd signed up for. I didn't want to spend my career in an immaculate confection of white cloth and gold braid, I wanted to be out there crawling in mud; I wanted to get dirt under my fingernails.

Ahead of our posting I was told that I was going to be transferred to the close observation platoon. I hadn't really been thinking about becoming part of the COP. It was usually more senior, experienced soldiers who joined them, because they had the job of doing the more complex, dangerous reconnaissance work.

But I think they recognised that I had something, and that I was absolutely dedicated to soldiering, so I got assigned there – though I made them promise I could return to my rifle company once we'd got back to the mainland. I loved being with my mates and wasn't ready to leave them behind. Not yet, anyway.

I went out to Northern Ireland for a six-week course where they attempted to teach me all the ways in which the counter-terrorism work I was about to embark on differed from the Cold War combat I'd been trained for. I learned what was known as the A–Z of recognising people, so we could identify the senior IRA we were there to observe. I remember them now, almost as if it were a catechism. A was age, B was build, D was distinguishing marks, E was elevation. Sometimes, I still find myself looking at people and trying to assess them using this framework. I guess old habits die hard.

We were taught about the IRA's command structure, and about the patterns in which they operated. What was never that clearly explained to us was exactly what we were doing in Ireland, or why. Perhaps they didn't think that the squaddies on the ground needed to know, or they thought that the complexities of a conflict with roots that reached back centuries would elude us. And they could have been right; maybe we didn't need to have our heads stuffed with that kind of thing.

¤

We arrived in South Armagh in the winter of 1984, a rural part of the country in which small villages were dotted among rolling fields that were divided up by towering hedgerows. Perhaps it didn't actually rain every day, but it certainly seemed to me as if it did. The land that wasn't farmed was astonishingly green, at least once spring had come, with vegetation growing so thickly that there were times when it could feel like you were operating in the jungle.

There was a reason that it was known as Bandit Country. It was in the nationalist heartland. People there had been fighting against the British since the beginning of the century, or for over a thousand years, depending on how you counted. There was an area of maybe two square kilometres, surrounding the village of Crossmaglen, in which more British soldiers had died than in any other patch of land since the Second World War. It was here that we would be stationed.

They hated us, really *hated* us. And they appeared to be doing everything they could to make it known that they didn't want us there. This might just be a matter of refusing to engage with us; they'd ignore you when you tried to be friendly, ostentatiously pretending you weren't there even if you were standing right next to them. Or they might give you abuse as you walked past on a day patrol, shouting 'Go back home' at us. The air was thick with their resentment and anger. Walls were daubed with the Irish tricolour, road signs would have graffiti scribbled on them announcing 'Sniper Works Here' or celebrating the number of British soldiers that had been killed.

I seemed to get singled out for more grief than anyone. I remember one Irish guy turning to me, his face snarled up with hate, but also disbelief: 'Why are you here, soldier boy? Why are *you* here?'

I understood enough to know that we were there, in theory, as neutrals, to help keep the peace. But it was sort of natural that we tended to gravitate towards the Protestants. When you crossed over into their areas it wasn't unusual to be greeted by someone waving the Union flag or offering you tea and cake. Although, alongside this, we knew about the atrocities that the so-called loyalist paramilitaries – the Ulster Defence Association and the Shankill Butchers – were responsible for. An atrocity is an atrocity. In the same way, I hated the IRA but I didn't hate Catholics. I mean, I didn't like being spat on, but I could see they were just normal people trying to get on with their lives as best they could.

We knew that the Catholics were often treated like second-class citizens. It was obvious; you could see it without having to look too hard. They didn't have the same money spent on their estates; they faced discrimination in almost every aspect of their lives. I started to ask myself how different their situation was from the sorts of things experienced by people in Britain who had the same colour skin as I did. I was thinking, *My dad used to get spat at, these people are being called 'dirty gypsies', isn't that the same?* The National Front were still marching through Britain's streets, cities were being torn up by rioters who felt as if they had been abused and neglected for too long.

And the crazy thing was, no matter how accomplished a soldier I was, at that time I'd not have been able to join the Scots Guards, the unit we had replaced. In fact, you wouldn't have seen a Black face in any of Britain's Guards regiments, which meant that every soldier back then outside Buckingham Palace, or participating in Trooping the Colour, would have been white. Officially, since 1968 it had been possible for anyone to serve anywhere in the armed forces; in practice, it was just never done.

To a certain extent, then, I could appreciate why they could not understand that a man like me was wearing that uniform. But then I was the son of a Black man who thought it was important to embrace the culture of the country he'd moved to. He'd come back from the pub, pour himself a last drink and make me stand up to attention when the National Anthem was played at the end of the day's TV programming.

I am proud to be British, and I'm proud to have served Queen and country. Symbols like the Union Jack are too important to be left in the hands of pot-bellied, boozed-up skinheads on their way to do a bit of 'Paki-bashing'. They're happy to sink ten pints at the football and bully whatever minority they see first, but would they even last a day in the military?

It's my flag, my country too. The Union Jack was on parade with us every morning when I was in the army; it flew above all of our camps. It really got to me when I saw these Nazis parading beneath it. I used to think: *How dare these fat, beer-drinking bovver boys? How dare they?*

That's why I also resent people who criticise the flag, saying it represents slavery, or colonialism. We should learn from our history, but we can't change it. Sometimes I think that hearing this is just as bad for a Black kid, growing up confused, trying to figure themselves out. I don't want them put off having the career I had, because that also means them being cut off from having all the opportunities it gave me. It means that we risk ending up divided against ourselves. I've never wanted that.

So maybe I could have said this, or something like it, to that Irish man who yelled at me in South Armagh. But I wasn't sure I could articulate it properly as we stood there on that freezing, windswept street, overlooked by graffiti boasting about how many of my comrades had been killed. Instead I just looked at him for a second, then mumbled that I was 'just doing my job'.

☐

There was no clear boundary between the people who you could rely on and trust, and those who wanted to hurt you. Everyone here looked the same; the terrorists didn't walk around clutching AK-47s or draped in Irish flags. They were just normal-looking men and women, often as young as me. One or two were pointed out to us as we conducted checkpoints. I remember looking at one, a slight boy with pasty skin and an ugly ginger mullet and thinking, *There's nothing to him.* At first it's almost comical to consider someone like that as your adversary. But as time went on I felt my nerves being scratched away by the thought that anybody could be potentially a bomb-maker, or carrying a gun, or passing information on to terrorists, or just silently hoping that I'd be the next body going back to the mainland.

We were so close to the border that the IRA could take potshots at us from the safety of the Republic. Groups of their active service units (ASUs) – the members of their organisation charged with carrying out attacks – roamed around, sometimes in groups as large as 18 men. Elsewhere in the province they did what they could to stay hidden; here they *wanted* to be seen.

The South Armagh Brigade of the IRA, allegedly led by Thomas 'Slab' Murphy, a local farmer whose property sprawled across the border, was one of the most notorious elements within the nationalist movement. Over the course of the Troubles they were directly responsible for the deaths of more than 165 members of the British security forces. There were thousands of troops stationed in this small stretch of the United Kingdom, and yet it still felt lawless, as if we were never fully in control.

We always had in our heads that threat the IRA had issued in the wake of their failed attack on Margaret Thatcher: 'We only have to be lucky once, you will have to be lucky always.'

Everything about the territory felt treacherous. We didn't live in barracks, we lived in mortar-proofed forts – ugly assemblies of corrugated iron and concrete that towered above the locals' small houses and cottages. They'd had to stop sending armoured vehicles down there because they were just being blown up by mines that were detonated either by remote or using a wire that went back across the border. The British government had effectively ceded roads to the terrorists. Instead we'd be dropped by a helicopter that would always do its best to make as quick an exit as it could. We always hoped that the pilots flying the Wessexes would be from the army rather than the RAF because the army guys would collect you no matter what, while the RAF would often bail if there was poor weather.

It was safer, but everything like this underlined how separate we were from the human beings we lived alongside. The threat against us shaped all of our movements. We rarely walked on roads, and never in straight lines, instead zigzagging over the ground in case a sniper was watching us.

Every journey took longer than it should have, because every hundred metres or so you'd have to find your way across another hedgerow or field. I climbed a lot of fences, because we knew that the gaps between hedges were often mined. You could tell someone who'd been in Ireland for a while because their combat trousers were covered in patches from where the barbed wire had ripped them. Nobody liked getting splinters in their arse, although you sometimes got a laugh when you saw a mate topple off a fence, dragged over it by the heavy load on their back.

Even the walking itself was hard work. The constant rain turned the soil into a quagmire that sucked at your boots. There was cow shit everywhere and bushes tugged at your clothes.

◻

The COP commander, Sergeant Ray Cross, was ten years older than me. He was huge but softly spoken, a real gentle giant. You couldn't miss him: his big bald head was ringed by light ginger hair, which was complemented by a long, drooping, Mexican-style moustache that sat in the middle of his slightly chubby face. But he was a good guy, really knowledgeable; his presence alone made me feel safer. He used to refer to our unit as the A-Team, after the popular show. He called me B.A. Baracus, which was ridiculous if you actually looked at me. Fit as I was, I was half his size, and I'm not sure I've even been in a room with that much jewellery, let alone worn it.

There were four of us in the patrol: a commander, his second in command, a radio-operator and a machine-gunner. That was my role. It meant I ended up carrying more equipment than anyone else. The machine-gun itself was an ancient piece of kit, essentially a minimally updated version of the Bren gun used in the Second World War – that tour would be the last time I ever saw one. Along with that I was burdened by vast quantities of ammunition and various different scopes, including a foot-long night-vision sight. It was all so heavy, I remember that when I took it off at the end of patrols, the relief from the pressure meant that I'd suddenly feel as if I was floating.

The ever-present threat of being blown up meant that alongside our weapons we carried electronic countermeasure (ECM) equipment. These ungainly boxes sprouting long antennae were designed to intercept the signals being sent by a terrorist trying to detonate a bomb remotely. We usually had a couple with us. There was a race between us and the terrorists, each side trying to progress to something better in order to get an edge. The one I had with me was silent, but my mate carried one that emitted a beep.

Not long after we'd got to South Armagh we were sent to a crossroads following intelligence that suggested an IRA unit was going to plant homemade explosives under its culvert. The idea was that we would catch them in the act.

It was a freezing January day. The crossroads itself felt desolate. Winter had stripped the trees of their leaves so that they loomed, dark and spidery above us.

Suddenly my mate's machine started chattering through his headphones. He looked up at us: 'My alarm's going off, I'm getting a positive reading.' I felt a pulse of fear. I was chilled by the idea that somebody, not far away from us, was trying to blow us to pieces. I whipped my head round and stared into the fields around us, as if by doing so I might be able to spot our ambushers.

Ray radioed through back to the Scots Guards who were still operating out of our new headquarters. 'Somebody's trying to blow us up.'

'Don't worry,' they told him. 'It's not a bomb, it's probably just a nearby electricity pylon.'

But the device carried on whining insistently. We checked the equipment again, and the message it was giving was unambiguous. Ray radioed again, but was put off with the same reassuring message: we've been here for months, there's always false alarms in this area.

Nevertheless, we got out of the area, a helicopter picked us up, and we thought no more of it. A week later Ray called me over. 'Look at this,' he said, thrusting a photograph into my hands, 'we should be angels now.'

For a second or two I was baffled. 'What are you on about?' Then I looked at the photograph. Somebody had dug up the crossroads we'd been lying on. They had uncovered barrels and barrels of the fertiliser the IRA used to make their homemade bombs. We'd been saved by our ECM; without that we'd have been eviscerated – we wouldn't have stood a chance.

◻

A large part of our role in the COP was watching homes and farms near the border that had been identified as having links to the IRA.

If we weren't inserted by helicopter we might be dropped off in an unmarked van that anybody watching would have thought was owned by a civilian. There was something terrifying about being stuck in this tight, stuffy windowless space, unable to tell whether anyone had observed you leaving the camp and followed you.

One way of avoiding this was to make sure we were dropped off a couple of kilometres from our destination. We'd make our way through the night, rain splashing our faces and spilling down the backs of our uniform, ensuring that even before we'd made camp we were soaked through. This was 1984, before Gore-Tex had been adopted by the British Army. Our journey would be followed by a rapid setting up of our post to make sure we were ready by dawn. This would be our home for ten days and nights, after which we'd be relieved. Unless we thought we'd been compromised, in which case we'd have to call in a helicopter and bug out.

We'd make observation posts under the dense green hedgerows that crisscrossed the area's rich farmland. They were primitive dwellings made of chicken-wire and our waterproof camouflage ponchos, laid over a hollow that we scraped out of the soil. They were a metre high and maybe two metres wide, with room for the four of us and our gear, but little else. Once we were in place, we'd begin our surveillance. There would always be two of us on watch: one observing what went on in front of us, another facing the other way to ensure that nobody could surprise us from the rear.

Hours would stretch by with not even the slightest movement. We recorded everything. What time did the milkman turn up? What was the registration of the blue Ford Sierra that arrived at 8.12am? We'd strain our eyes trying to pick out the driver's age and build. If we had a camera we'd snap photo after photo. The watching would continue even after night had fallen. A light coming on in a particular room could have significance that we didn't appreciate, so we'd make a note. It wasn't our job to interpret the intelligence, or judge what was important; we were just there to collect it.

Sometimes one of us would sneak closer to the house to get a better look. You'd crawl across the dark ground, the smell of damp soil filling your nostrils, the grass soaking your uniform, before returning to the observation post before dawn. In some ways this chance to move was welcome. The oppressive, cramped silence of the hedgerow was agony. But the further you got from the relative safety of your hide, the more you made yourself vulnerable to any ASU patrolling the area.

There were just two sleeping bags. We'd swap every two or three hours. The idea was that the men in the sleeping bags would get a chance to rest, although when it came to my turn, while I was always exhausted, there was still so much adrenaline charging through my system that I'd rarely manage to doze off. We knew how isolated we were, and how vulnerable our proximity to the border made us.

Somewhere, nearby, there would be another patrol. We were supposed to be supporting each other, but especially on those nights when the mist came down, enveloping everything, they felt very far away. To all intents and purposes, we were alone amid the green leaves and freezing cold air. If something went wrong, we'd be dead before our neighbours knew anything about it.

Anything that approached us was a potential threat. A tractor trundling through the field next to us might be on its way to inspect the hedgerow we were hiding in, because something about it had struck its driver as strange, or different. If that happened, we knew we'd be in trouble – the local farmers, many of whom were IRA sympathisers, were as much of a threat to us as the IRA themselves. A nosy cow might unwittingly give away our location. That's why we existed in almost total silence, and also why we made sure that everything that went in with us came out again: it had to look untouched. What sawed away at my nerves was that it was never possible to be certain whether we'd been spotted. We might only discover that a nationalist farmer had seen us and informed the IRA once we found ourselves in an ambush.

It just needed a farmer to hang around near us for a few minutes longer than I'd anticipated to set off a rush of anxiety.

◻

Being the new boy had other drawbacks beyond having to carry a heavy machine-gun.

Given how tight our space was, we compromised on what we brought in. We didn't take as many rations as we might need for a mission that involved more physical exertion. But we did get containers of fresh water every few days. I was never allowed to go to pick them up; that was the commander's privilege. He got to stretch his legs while the rest of us were left wondering whether our limbs would ever stop aching. For hours after the end of each mission I'd feel like an old man.

It wasn't just the cramped conditions, there was also the damp that seemed to seep into your bones. It was almost always pissing down and our ponchos could only provide so much cover. The water would inevitably find the gap in the fabric, or else there would be horizontal rain that spat in our faces.

We'd chew the soggy cheese and tomato or egg mayonnaise sandwiches that were the mainstays of our army rations. The worst were the oranges that would become, after a day in the frigid countryside of South Armagh, so cold that each segment you ingested seemed to lower your body temperature. This was the reward you got for struggling to peel them with red-raw freezing hands.

We urinated into one of the gallon-container bottles that we'd brought water in. I hated this. When the container got too full you'd find your dick touching the stale, stinking liquid inside and you'd think, *I'm touching someone else's piss: I don't know if I'll ever be clean again.* We defecated into cling film, which we wrapped up. It was then passed to me to put in a black plastic sack, which was kept in my bag. By the end I'd have ten days' worth of four men's shit. Everyone else left with a pack lighter than when they'd come in. Mine was heavier. Although one time it was so cold that I held on to my comrade's wrapped-up shit for a few seconds longer than I normally would: disgusting as it was, that package also warmed my hands.

The atmosphere in there was fetid. We emerged stinking and unshaved. The loadmasters ushering us onto the helicopters taking us to safety would blench as our foul smell crept up their nostrils. But what could we do?

We'd come back to the headquarters and be told that we looked like a bunch of gypsies and to try to get some rest before we were called out again.

◻

The clue to what we were there to do was in the title of our unit. We were there to observe. If our superiors felt that something was about to go off, they'd turn elsewhere. There was one operation where we got extracted after just a couple of days because the targets had been seen with bags that the man who'd been on watch thought might contain weapons. We got pulled out at night-time. As we started our debrief in an anonymous room in our headquarters a pack of scruffy but strong-looking geezers with big moustaches and beards came in.

This wasn't my first encounter with the SAS. On my COP training course a wiry old major – he was probably in his fifties but to me he looked as if he was 70, at least – put in a couple of appearances. On one of them he took us out on a run along a nearby beach. We ran and ran across the dunes, with him in front, barely appearing to break sweat, and the rest of us stumbling and puffing behind. We eventually came to an exhausted halt. Breezily, as if he'd just been for a little post-breakfast stroll, he said: 'OK, same again tomorrow.'

I remember looking at this slender slip of a man and thinking, *God almighty, where's that come from?* But it was obvious he had something.

The same was true with these guys. Even though I didn't speak to them – they confined themselves to a quiet word with Ray Cross – I could see that they were different. Their uniform was different, none of them were wearing standard issue boots, and they projected an aura of complete confidence. To tell the truth, I was slightly intimidated by them. They were hard *men*, and I was just a kid. At the same time, I felt a stab of jealousy that they got brought in to do all the 'good jobs'. I thought to myself, *I want some of this.*

There wasn't much time to stew on this thought. Despite famous successes like their participation in the siege at the Iranian Embassy a few years before, the SAS remained a shadowy, mysterious element within the armed forces. Even if I'd wanted to join them then, I'm not sure if I'd have known how to go about putting myself forward.

And, anyway, I had more immediate concerns. Being in the COP took me away from my mates in the Staffordshire Regiment, like my best friend Proctor, or Prock, who lived over the road from me in Bentilee and was in B Company. Like me, Prock was a Stoke fan, and a skinhead who loved the same music. Looking back now, you'd say he was a bit of a lad, but he was always joking, always happy. I didn't get much of either when I was sitting there, cold, bored and afraid in an observation post. So I missed them and always tried to catch up with the rest of the Staffords boys whenever I got the occasion to do so. One of those occasions would mark me more deeply than almost any experience in my life.

I'll never forget that morning because it was one of the rare days when it didn't rain. Somehow that seemed to make the atmosphere a bit less oppressive. Even better than that, because we were off to reconnoitre an area where we were considering setting up an observation post later that night, we'd managed to loop through Crossmaglen and link up with B Company at the headquarters where we lived in little blocks where our beds were stacked three-high, as if we were in a submarine. We caught them just before they went out on a patrol. It felt good to stand there in the open air with them, our faces warmed by weak spring sunshine as we chatted.

They told me that there'd been an incident a couple of days before when a patrol had literally bumped into an ASU, each side as surprised as the other by the encounter. There was a short gun battle, which ended with the capture of one of the IRA men and a chunk being shot out of the ear of one of our officers.

This meant that the fields around the village should have been put out of bounds until the risk engineers with all their metal detectors and dog handlers had gone in to check it – the IRA could have been there putting in improvised explosive devices (IEDs).

That was the theory, anyway, but the company's commander was a Major Wilkinson, a snobbish, difficult character who I'd never had much time for. He was a demon for drill and room inspections but never seemed to like actual soldiering that much. I found myself shrinking a bit every time I saw him. Someone, years later, pointed out that he looked like Mr Burns from *The Simpsons*. That felt about right to me. His wife was just as bad. She insisted on us ordinary soldiers calling her *Mrs* Major Wilkinson. To them we were just oiks.

Major Wilkinson did it his own way. His attitude was, *this area is my responsibility, so it's up to me to take a look round it.* As the COP readied ourselves for our own patrol, we watched as Major Wilkinson took the sergeant major and the company clerk with him, leading the way – more troops and a couple of dog-handlers trailed a little way behind them. Too far away to be of much use if anything happened. The company clerk was Lance Corporal Steve Anderson. Everyone liked him – he was known as one of the good guys. He was a few years older than me, and had made a point of welcoming me when I arrived in Gibraltar, showing me the ropes. I wouldn't have settled into the company half as quickly if it hadn't been for him. I knew he was a married father, and that his wife had another on the way. As he passed me I smiled and waved before returning to my kit.

Once we were ready, we headed off towards the border. We loped comfortably through the lush green countryside while above us heavy white clouds scudded across the sky. The dry weather was a welcome change; I thought about how nice it would be, just for *once*, to sit in our observation post without water dripping on my head. I shifted the machine-gun that was cradled into my arms to a slightly more comfortable position. That's when I heard the explosion. We all whipped around. About 600 metres away we saw a thick plume of oily black smoke. At almost the same time our radios burst into life. 'B Company has just had contact.' There was something different about the tone of the speaker's voice, a kind of compressed grief. It was clear that something terrible had happened. We were told that a bomb had exploded and there was one fatality and a number of injuries. For the moment, we knew nothing else. We stayed put.

I felt sick with fear and disbelief. Instantly I found myself saying, almost like a prayer, 'Not Proc, not Proc, please not my mate from across the road.'

This gave way quickly to a pure, white hatred. We'd been given the victim's ZAP number, a combination of letters from their surname and digits from their army number that identified them, but didn't for the moment recognise it. I realised it didn't matter who had been killed; I was overcome by a desire for immediate revenge. I've never before or since felt this kind of rage. I was shaking with adrenaline. All I wanted was for a couple of terrorists to stray into my sights as they rushed away from the site of their crime.

Come on, you bastards. Come on, you twats. I just wanted one shot. I lay there, waiting, helpless anguish and fury swilling inside me. Nobody came.

A little later I was told that the bloke who'd been killed was Steve Anderson. I felt almost sick with anguish, but there wasn't time to grieve. Within a matter of hours, I was sitting in a scraped-out hollow beneath a hedgerow, still trying to process what had happened. I felt completely alone with my thoughts. As kind as Ray Cross was to me, neither he nor the other guys in my patrol had known Steve that well, so they weren't as torn up as I was.

Ten days later, when I was able to see the lads in B Company, I found out what had happened. The bomb had taken both his legs and a finger off. Killed him instantly. Major Wilkinson went through a gap in a hedge, followed by another guy, and then Steve Anderson, who stepped on a pressure plate. The dog handler behind him was blinded.

My mates seethed with helpless rage at the situation. Their commander had made a terrible mistake, the IRA had killed one of their mates, but there was nothing much they could do.

There was another casualty a little while later: someone else, who I also knew, got shot in the head. It was hard to stop thinking about them. From that point on, every observation mission felt more charged with danger. I felt permanently jumpy and on edge – even the smallest noises could alarm me.

I had hellish nights straining my ears to try to work out whether the noise I could hear in the dark and mist around me was just a couple of cows working their way through the nearby grass, or something more sinister. I'd poke my night-vision goggles (NVGs) out and all I'd see was a yellow-green blur. There would be a fresh wave of adrenaline and I'd wonder if this was something worth waking Ray Cross over – unlike me, he managed to sleep happily when it wasn't his turn to be on stag. *What do I do? Is that an ASU? Do they know we're here? Are they coming for us?* I'd be convinced that there were ten men creeping through the undergrowth, coming ever closer to our post.

I'd make frantic calculations as I tried to steady my frayed nerves. I didn't want to be ambushed, but nor was I that anxious to get a reputation as a flapper. I remember how one night I heard sounds close to our observation post. In the dark it was hard to be sure of anything. *Was that a man's boot squelching through mud? Was that the chink of a rifle knocking against a belt?* I thought about all the stories of men, like me, who'd already died in this sodden stretch of countryside. My fingers gently released my weapon's safety catch. Whatever was making that noise, I was ready. Then, inevitably, there was a gentle lowing, and the ripping sound of grass being torn out of the soil by hungry cows.

¤

The anxiety leached into everything we did. At times I'd be on patrol in broad daylight and would suddenly be struck by the realisation that I was right by the border and the only thing I had to protect my body were two six-inch by eight-inch pieces of armour plate, one on my back, the other covering my heart. If I got hit by a sniper, they would be just enough to prevent my guts slopping out of my stomach. If I stepped on an IED they'd be useless.

It became hard to stop thinking about snipers. We knew that they frequently operated in the area. One could have me, or one of my mates, in his sights at any minute. Your mind does strange things then. I would find myself wondering whether he'd shoot me or the radio operator first. Ludicrously, when these sorts of ideas started to clamber into my mind, I'd lower my machine-gun a couple of inches so it offered protection for my groin. *If he shoots, at least I'll be able to save them.* But even this brief moment of respite would be followed, quickly, by darker speculation. *What does it feel like to get shot? I could get shot at any time. My next step could be my last.*

76

One incident in particular stands out for me. We had been sent into the Derrybeg Estate in Newry – another staunch nationalist area – watching an IRA quartermaster. The estate had only been built in 1963 but just 20 years on it had become a neglected ghost town. A third of its houses were empty.

The army's engineers routinely searched derelict properties for any weapons or equipment the IRA might have tried to hide. Our unit joined a group of them sifting through the crumbling interiors of an abandoned house in a dreary terraced building. Through the front door went 16 men. Only 12 came out. Four of us stayed inside as our comrades boarded the windows and doors back up.

We secreted ourselves in an upstairs room and did not leave for another ten days. I spent a lot of time at the front of the building, looking out with my scope through a couple of holes that had been drilled into the corrugated iron that had been used to cover the windows. I'd take photos of anybody coming in or out of the quartermaster's house, though I never saw the man himself.

We had been told which terrorists to look out for. If we saw any with weapons, that'd be our cue to call out the emergency groups, who'd try to snatch them red-handed.

We heard every noise made by the men in the house next to ours, who we knew were terrorists too – muffled talk that would occasionally be interrupted by loud shouts. We had to stay completely silent. We avoided even moving around, for fear that we'd set the floorboards creaking. When we spoke, it was in whispers. It was strange how quickly you got used to this. So much so that when you started speaking 'normally' again after the ten days it felt as if you were screaming at the top of your voice.

Our days were organised in a similar pattern to our existence in the hedgerows: four hours on, four hours off, with the relieved soldier climbing into the warm sleeping bag their comrade had just left. Once again we found ourselves pissing into a container and wrapping our shit up in plastic bags.

And just like in the hedgerows, every unusual noise seemed to carry danger. One day, as I stared through the little aperture in the boarded-up window, the corrugated iron shuddered deafeningly as it was struck by some kind of missile. *Fuck, we're being shot at.* I pressed my eye to the metal, which was still reverberating from the impact, expecting to see a balaclava-clad terrorist clutching an Armalite. Instead, I saw a ragged kid strolling away nonchalantly after having heaved a rock at what he thought was an empty building. I slumped back to the floor and waited for my furiously beating heart to slow down.

Mostly, though, it was mind-numbing. We couldn't cook anything, because we didn't want to give our presence away by making telltale smells, so existed off cold rations like tins of beans and bacon, or corned beef, as well as plain brown biscuits or, as a treat, Garibaldis. There were no fresh vegetables or fruit. Time passed so slowly that I would try to entertain myself by putting boiled sweets in my mouth and seeing how long it would take for them to dissolve.

We had nothing to read; my only luxury was a Walkman with a pair of tiny little headphones – all we were allowed to take with us. I listened to the same Thompson Twins album over and over as I shivered in my sleeping bag, trying, and failing, to get some rest.

You never got used to the idea that there were terrorists on the other side of the walls.

When tedium and terror get twisted up like that it can do something to your mind, especially when you're young. It can tip you into a dark place.

□

I came home for four weeks on leave and went straight on the piss with my best mate. A couple of 19-year-olds having the time of their life in Blackpool. Listening to The Style Council's 'Long Hot Summer' and David Bowie's 'Let's Dance'. Drinking all day. But that wasn't the whole story. One evening, I got onto the bus to go into town to see my mates. The conductor told me how much the fare was. My mind suddenly froze. I couldn't remember how to count the money, I just stared at him. 'Come on. What's wrong with you?' he said, trying to jog me out of whatever daze he thought I was in. But I remained frozen. He took the money from my hands and moved on, before I sat down.

Not long afterwards I broke down a bit and cried in my parents' kitchen, which terrified my mum, who I'd told what had happened. She insisted on me seeing a doctor, who didn't seem as bothered. 'Just stop drinking so much,' he told me cheerfully. That was a relief. I told myself, *I'm all right*.

79

After that, I *was* all right. Sort of. I'd still have scary little moments when I heard a bang, but I decided not to dwell on what had happened, or to open up and talk about how it had made me feel. There wasn't counselling or anything like that, either in the aftermath of what happened in Northern Ireland, or at any point later.

I took that brisk attitude to trauma and grief with me throughout my time in the army and into the SAS. Whatever happened on missions, no matter how brutal or upsetting, I'd deliberately force the memories to the back of my mind, cramming them into a space that became more and more cramped over the passage of time. These were things that I never wanted to think about again. I reckoned if they were out of sight, they wouldn't have the power to trouble me.

That approach was probably quite similar to most of the blokes in the regiment. If someone died in an accident, or on an operation, we wouldn't really speak about what we'd seen, or what emotions it might have stirred up in us. Then we'd have a night when anyone who was back at the SAS headquarters in Hereford would spend a night drinking and bidding for the dead man's gear. We didn't really want it; it was just making sure that their family had money. It was a case of: *Now we move on. Remember the good times. Have a laugh. But we have to go on. He'd done something that he enjoyed.*

I did the same when my dad died. 'Quickly, Mum, let's get rid of his stuff.' I don't think that was the right mindset to have: getting everything sorted as quickly as I could, telling my mum,

'You don't need this any more. Put it in the garden shed. You don't want too much to remind you.'

Later, years later, she had a go at me about it. And I remember thinking, *Yeah, she was right. Why* did *I do that?*

There's no handbook for dealing with grief. Bad experiences aren't always accompanied by lessons. Still, in years to come, I'd find that my approach to discomforting thoughts, which helped me get from one mission to the next, would have its own complications.

4

WE'LL SEE WHO'S BOSS

In 1986 we were posted to Fallingbostel, Germany, where we joined 7th Armoured Brigade, the Second World War's infamous Desert Rats.

The base had originally been built as accommodation for the SS soldiers who guarded Belsen, the death camp, whose remnants were only a few kilometres away. Next to the camp was an old station which had been the last stop on the train line. After this, the prisoners were driven in trucks to be gassed or worked to death. We'd been told that Russian soldiers had just been left to die in the fields around us. Knowing this made the whole area eerie. When we first arrived we noticed that the plaster on one of the buildings was crumbling. If you looked closer, it was possible to see a fragment of a black painted wing. We pulled a bit more of the plaster off, revealing a huge eagle, its talons resting on a swastika. Sometimes we'd run on the old train tracks, or across the cobblestones that surrounded the barracks, and I'd get a chilling flash of what it must have been like just 40 years before.

Even without this grim history, Fallingbostel made a pretty cold, bleak home. The sparse greenery that had been planted here and there around the vast camp could do little to soften its hard, utilitarian feel. The windows were small, the rooms were basic; it felt and looked like a prison.

But to begin with, I enjoyed my time there. This was mostly due to the fact that my company, B Company, was now being led by a new officer, Major Sampson (this is not his real name, for obvious reasons, I've given him a pseudonym), who'd taken over in 1985, while we had been stationed in Colchester.

There had been a buzz about him before we'd even met him because we'd learned that he'd come from the SAS. This made him unusual in the Staffords, because we didn't really have much of a track record of our boys getting into the special forces. As far as I knew, since the new regiment had been formed in 1959 (combining the North and South Staffordshire Regiments), just one guy had made it through selection, and that had been in 1974, way before my time.

But Sampson was brilliant, a total inspiration to me because he seemed different from any other officer I'd served under. In fact, he was unlike any soldier I'd ever encountered. He was a big dark-haired athletic man, perhaps as tall as six foot two, in his late thirties. Like the SAS soldiers I'd encountered before, his face was dominated by a drooping, Mexican-style moustache. And yet what you noticed first was the way he seemed to bound rather than walk. It was the first sign of his energy and unconventionality.

Most of our officers had been fit, but Sampson was unbelievable. He never tired, no matter how hard the task, or how long we were out for. Everything had a purpose, too. He made us run in our gas masks, which was horrible, obviously, but it was a preparation for our posting in Germany. It was still the Cold War, there was still the fear that one day the Soviets would try to sweep into

Western Europe, and we needed to be ready for whatever sort of conflict they wanted to start. The other big thing was that he did it with us – not every officer would have. They were more likely to watch as you tackled an assault course. This was a time when the senior officers still had a batman – a little runner to clean his clothes and polish his boots. They'd have their own drivers too. One of the duties we had sometimes was to go and be a waiter in the officers' mess. I always offered to swap when it was my turn on the rotation. I'd be willing to take on someone else's guard duty, stand out in the cold and wet for hours at a time. Anything was better than spending the night looking after somebody's blinking wife, pouring them fine wines as they snapped at me: 'Do this', 'Get me that'. I hadn't joined the army for *that*.

A lot of officers patronised us. On formal occasions we were reminded that our wives shouldn't wear skirts that finished above their knees. They acted as if we were so dumb we wouldn't know how to behave at a formal occasion.

There was an expectation that people who came from poor council estates would always keep those values and tastes. There'd be shock from the officers if they saw one of their privates at, say, the theatre: 'What are *you* doing here? Why aren't you at a pub?'

Those sorts of officers favoured the guys who bullshitted them, the 'yes sir, no sir' men, and devoted most of their attention to room inspections and perfecting drill. I think because they'd calculated that these were the best ways of impressing their superiors.

That wasn't Sampson's way. He was only interested in one question: what are you like as a *soldier*? If you could operate in the field, if you could shoot, move and communicate, then he was happy. You'd see his dark eyes, which occasionally twitched in a slightly disconcerting way, sparkle.

It was exciting to be around someone who thought differently.

There was an exercise where we were sent to an open field to dig trenches. Anyone else would have left it there; we'd have just waited in the trenches for the next order. But Sampson had us collecting branches from the nearby woods then fashioning them into stakes that we planted in the ground. It was like we were medieval archers waiting for French knights to charge. We had absolutely no idea why we were doing this, until Sampson explained: 'Right, guys, this is in case they decide to come by helicopter.' And then it dawned on me: *God almighty, they won't be able to land there.*

Another time, we were supposed to be assaulting an 'enemy' position. When we were about 800 metres away, he ordered us to start crawling. It took us almost the entire night to reach our target, but we sneaked up and took them by surprise.

It was hard not to compare this to an experience with our previous officer, a tubby Labrador-walker who rarely left his office. That time, on another exercise, he had the company walking together, in a big bunch, down the middle of a road. I was 19, I barely knew a thing, and yet even I was thinking, *We shouldn't be doing this.* Sure enough, within minutes an 'enemy' unit attacked us, and the umpires ruled that we'd all been killed. It was so demoralising, and quickly became embarrassing when our officer started protesting in his strident, plummy voice.

'We're *not* dead. We. Are. Not. Dead.'

The other great thing about Sampson was that he recognised potential, and wanted you to achieve everything he believed you were capable of. Just before Sampson joined, although I was already a lance corporal, I was beginning to get itchy feet and was considering becoming a gym instructor. I basically wanted to do something a bit more physical. So I went on a six-week PT course, did well, and returned thinking that I'd found the route I was going to take.

Sampson had other ideas. 'You're going on your corporals' course,' he told me, talking briskly, in a way that suggested he wasn't really expecting to have an argument. I took my cue from him, but to be honest I was surprised. Usually you had to wait quite a bit longer before you took that step. However, the faith Sampson showed in me was electrifying. I passed the course and he made me straight up to corporal. I had just turned 20 and now I was in charge of eight blokes.

I'd have followed Sampson to the end of the world, and was cut up when he was sent on an external posting after two years. Officers tended to shift around quite a lot, sometimes going to another unit to get experience, or to teach at staff college. However, I now had a new sense of my horizons. He'd inspired me to believe that maybe I could take my place among the best of the best.

The fact that only a couple of our regiment had ever made it into the SAS didn't mean that lads from the Staffords weren't trying. There was a steady stream of guys, including a mate of mine, Dixie, who'd give it a go. But they all came back, often with horror stories. A couple made it as far as the second week of selection. This by itself was enough to give them an aura.

I started to consider putting my papers in too, so I had a conversation with a soldier who'd recently been sent back to us after the first week. 'I'm going for the SAS.'

He looked at me kindly, the way you might a kid who needs something obvious explaining to them. 'No, Mel, you can't do that. You won't be allowed.'

'Why's that?'

'You're Black.'

'What's that got to do with it?'

'You know they go undercover in Northern Ireland.'

'Yeah.' I'd heard that this happened.

'Well, there aren't many Black people in Northern Ireland, are there?' This was also true. 'You're hardly going to be able to sit in a Belfast bar and sneak information out of someone, are you?'

This made sense to me, so I quietly dropped the idea.

¤

With Sampson gone, I felt, for the first time, my enthusiasm for the army begin to wilt. I still wanted to be a soldier, I just didn't like the sort of soldiering that was being offered. I'd got an early sign of what our new lives as part of a mechanised infantry regiment would be like when, just before we deployed to Germany, I'd gone on an infantry training course and one of the other guys was from Fallingbostel. He'd been there for years, and the thing I noticed was that he wasn't a particularly good soldier on the ground. His kit wasn't great, his drills left a fair bit to be desired. Cautiously, we asked him about this, expecting him to be pissed off that we'd noticed. But he wasn't; he just explained that this was because he'd been operating out of an armoured fighting vehicle, where you didn't really need those skills.

They lived in what was, essentially, a heavily armoured caravan. Some people, the tankies, loved that. They enjoyed checking the oils and tinkering around with engines. For them, there was nothing better than being in the vehicle sheds. I didn't fancy that, I didn't want to be driven around the whole time, I had always been someone who preferred having my boots on the ground.

In many ways I was still the kid I'd been on the Bentilee estate, fizzing with energy. I'm a bit like a shark, I guess; I have to be moving all the time. Caravanning demoralised me. I started considering a move to the Foreign Legion, or the American Marines. I reckoned that either of them would give me the chance of finding the excitement and challenge I was after. What's the point of a uniform if you're not fighting in it? But, instead, I found something else that offered me what I was looking for so desperately: boxing.

❏

I'd done a bit of boxing when we'd been in Colchester, and enjoyed it, so when the opportunity to do it again in Germany came up, I jumped at the chance. As soon as he saw how fit and enthusiastic I was, our trainer, Staff Sergeant Rogers – a muscular, lean Scot with cropped ginger hair from the Army Physical Training Corps – made me captain of the team.

Boxing was a big thing in the army in the time. Every regiment would enter a huge cup competition. You'd start off fighting the units that were stationed close to you, then if you progressed you'd start travelling further and further. If your team lost, you'd be back in uniform, if you won you just carried on. You'd fight to be the best regiment in your region, then in the country where you were stationed, then in the entire army. With each new round, your opponents got tougher, because they too had vanquished a number of other units to get to this point. The grand final was broadcast live on army radio and TV.

Staff Sergeant Rogers had been posted to our regiment to look after our fitness and adventure-training activities. But his real passion was boxing – at one time he'd boxed for Scotland – and he pushed and pushed and pushed us, because he wanted us to behave as if we were professionals.

We trained eight hours a day, marked out by our special track-suits. We even ate separately from the other boys, and got better food. The feeling was that we needed these privileges because we were expected to work harder than anybody else. There were whistle sprints where you had to run as fast as you can: really tough circuit training. Sparring. Shadow-boxing. Skipping. Working in the bag room, or in a huge attic above the barracks, which was red hot in the summer, and barely cooler in the winter, when our coach would bring in massive heaters. Whatever the season, we emerged from our sessions ringing wet.

Everybody would be knackered, but after that I'd still go for an eight-mile jog, day in, day out. I forced myself to do it because I knew it would give me an edge; I needed to make up for in fitness what I lacked in skill. There were only three two-minute rounds. Perhaps the more polished fighters might have been able to take advantage if the bouts had unfolded in a more leisurely way. As it was, I reckoned that if I could go in with a flurry – bam, bam, bam, bam, bam – I could overwhelm them before their superior technique could be made to pay.

That intensity, the physical demands it makes on you, the thinking it requires – it's why I still love boxing so much. But, more than anything, it's the willpower you have to show. You have to tell yourself that you will not allow yourself to be beaten, no matter what. You have to be willing to be hurt, to take punishment in order to get the thing that you want.

It is as close to going into battle as you can get. That feeling of knowing that it's just you and another man fighting against each other, except that you're being watched by thousands of blokes in their best uniforms, screaming for blood. It was only three rounds, but it was full-on and I loved it.

◻

In 1987 we motored through the competition, smashing all-comers.

The matches that really stick in my memory were the last two that year, for very different reasons. In the semi-final I was matched with a guy from 50th Missile Regiment. Every team had nine boxers fighting at different weights – having an odd number of bouts ensured that there would always be a result. I was 71 kilograms and boxed at light middleweight, which put me fifth in the running order.

Usually Staff Sergeant Rogers would try to see our opponents fight before we went into the ring with them and he'd report back on their weaknesses and strengths. He had a great eye for the sport, so I always trusted his judgement.

But this time he refused to say much. When I asked him what he made of my opponent, he'd said, 'Yeah, he's all right. You just do as you do.' In retrospect, I should have realised that something was up.

I entered the gym where the bouts were being held to find it filled with thousands of men. One side of the hall was blokes from my regiment, another was blokes from his. Our officers sat in the same section as their counterparts in 50th Missile Regiment, intermingled in their red formal jackets.

The noise was almost deafening: a cacophony that bounced around the high walls of the gym then returned with added force. My regiment was in a raucous, hoarse-voiced competition with our opponents to see who could shout the loudest. I could hear my name being chanted. 'Melvyn, Melvyn, MELVYN.' Goose pimples ran up and down my arms.

I stood there for a second, soaking it all in. That moment never stopped being special: exciting and terrifying at the same time. Later, I'd feel that same intoxication before combat. And then the band started. We didn't have a ring walk, like you might see in a civilian bout. We didn't choose our own music to come out to. What we had was better: we were played out by our regimental band, who might be accompanied by their mascot.

If you were fighting a Scottish regiment, they'd have their bagpipes. A light infantry unit would have bugles. I remember the Royal Anglian Regiment, known as the poachers, would come out preceded by a man in country clothes, with rabbits hanging from his belt. The Welsh would have a goat. We had a Staffordshire terrier and a band with drums.

They'd start their clattering, bashing out rhythms that had accompanied the Staffords into battle for centuries. Somehow, even amid the chaos and shouting they were still loud. I loved the sharp snap and crash of wooden sticks hitting taut animal hide. This was when the nerves really started. I'd walk in, the drummers behind me, and then, for the few seconds it took to stride across the gymnasium, I would get this feeling, somewhere deep in my body, that I was a criminal on my way to be hanged. The ring loomed ahead of me like a scaffold. I could imagine them slipping the noose over my neck; I could almost feel the roughness of rope on my skin.

Most were still shouting my name, but others had broken into a popular regimental song:

She wore, she wore, she wore a yellow ribbon
She wore it for a Stafford who was far, far away
Far away, not far enough far away
Too fucking far
She wore it for a Stafford who was far, far away.

The blokes from the other regiment were doing the same. I could hear my opponent's name melding with their own songs.

Even as I climbed the steps I thought to myself, could not help believing, that I was about to be hanged. All I wanted was for the bell to ring, for the first few punches to be thrown. I don't remember any of the formalities that led up to the fight, just a rush of noise. Screams, yells, my name and his crashing against each other.

Clang. Suddenly I was no longer nervous, no longer aware of anything beyond the several hundred square feet of canvas in which I was fighting, lit powerfully from above by the lights hanging from the ceiling. It was like there was nobody else in the room but me and my opponent. Even the wall of sound that just seconds ago had threatened to deafen me had receded to almost nothing, with only the odd isolated shout breaking through.

Smithy was a white guy with close-cropped dark hair. He stood maybe an inch shorter than me, so I had a longer reach, but he was thickset, exuding power, and seemed to move constantly. I could see straight away that his footwork was good, probably better than anybody I'd faced before.

His skill meant he was able to punch through my guard. The first time one of his fists crashed into my torso it winded me instantly. The force and speed made me think, *God, I've been punched by four men at the same time.* He slammed one into my right side, then my left, followed by a crunch to my jaw. He was a whir of menace and intent. As I tried to gather myself there was another flurry. *He's good,* I thought. I started to fear I wouldn't be able to keep up with him. I was taking a lot of punishment and offering almost nothing in return. It was like I was scrabbling to get a grip on a mountain ledge as someone standing above me kicked at my fingers.

He hit me with a big punch to my stomach, a left hook, a right hook. I reeled away. Crash, he caught my jaw again. I thought, *Where's* that *come from?*

I lurched in his direction, trying to land even a glancing blow on him, I desperately needed to get some momentum, but he skipped away. He appeared to be operating at a completely different speed from me.

The bell clanged and I returned, stunned, my whole body vibrating with pain, to my corner. I could see Staff Sergeant Rogers looking at me, a concerned expression on his face, 'How are you doing?' he asked me. My ears were ringing so loudly I could barely hear him.

'Yeah, I'm all right.' I didn't really believe that, and my coach stared sceptically at me; we both knew I was in trouble. I'd never fought anyone like this.

The second round began like a continuation of the first. Smithy smashed me a couple of times. Then his fist hurtled into my jaw. I could instantly taste blood. There was that familiar feeling of shock in the lower half of my face, a sensation that is difficult to describe, though it's perhaps most similar to the tension that builds just before you sneeze.

My brain zigzagged with lightning. *Wow, I'm going to get it,* I thought, *I'm going to get sparked if I don't do* something *now.* I felt filled with the urge to try to grapple with him, or swing a wild punch in his direction. But dizzy and reeling as my head was, I knew that I had to suppress this impulse. The best thing I could do, at least for a handful of seconds, was nothing.

◻

I was always the kind of fighter who needed to take a couple of punches before I was able to get into my rhythm. It was like I needed that shock. Still, once I'd learned this about myself, I went on an amazing run in the ring. I won bout after bout.

I thought I was great. I thought nothing could stop me. And then somebody did.

The other guy got me right on the temple with a haymaker. My vision swirled and wobbled, and time slowed down into a sickening crawl as the referee gave me a count, which was interrupted by the bell. Somehow, I was still able to stand, I was too proud – or too stupid – to give up and yet I was too dazed to operate properly. A series of blows rained down on me. The fog in my head got thicker. I was done.

I came back from that experience smarter. I knew that next time, when I got smashed over the head and felt as if the world was spinning around me, the worst thing I could do was to try to fight through it. You need to make time for yourself. Far better to cover up, try to hold on for long enough for your head to right itself. If I needed to, I'd flick my gumshield out, because that was enough in amateur boxing to buy yourself a few seconds: the referee would have to stop the fight for long enough to give your gumshield a clean. Since then, I've always tried to find a still point, no matter how chaotic everything else is.

¤

On this occasion, I didn't need to resort to any tricks. It was enough to remind myself that I'd been in these positions before, I'd felt this shock before. I edged back on the canvas, dodging two swipes from Smithy, doing nothing more than keeping my guard up and my feet moving.

I waited for a couple of seconds, hoping he'd give me an opening. Then it came. A missed punch left him slightly off balance. I caught him, once, twice. That was when something changed. Suddenly, I had the momentum. Taking punches rather than delivering them seemed to demoralise him. I could sense that his energy was beginning to drain away, while I felt stronger than at any point during the entire fight. I started pummelling him, finding it easier and easier to land blows. In the first round, everything had rushed past me at an uncontrollable pace; now I had the time to pick my shots. When the end of the third round came, I knew I would walk out of that great echoing hall as the victor. A few minutes later, the judges confirmed this: I had won unanimously.

Later that night, as we drank together in the sergeants' mess, where we'd always go after regimental fights to be fed and plied with free beers, I found out a bit more about him.

He'd been fighting since he was a kid, and whatever ended up happening in this competition, he was going to head off to America to compete in the Golden Gloves, maybe the most prestigious amateur boxing event in the world. He was too good a boxer to be in the ring with us. By rights he shouldn't have been anywhere near us.

What saved me in that semi-final was that there were just three rounds. Skill mattered less than aggression and fitness. Smithy said that he'd never fought anybody fitter than me. I glowed with pride: there was almost nothing he could have said that would have made me prouder.

¤

We found ourselves up against the Paras in the final. As I entered the gym, I was greeted with the usual din. But, as I stood there, waiting for the signal to start my doomed convict's walk to the ring, I realised I could make out something else. Monkey noises. It was just a handful – every unit had its share of racists, just like in any walk of life – though obviously that didn't make it any better.

This wasn't the first time I'd experienced something like this. I'd heard the same derogatory noises from the Guards regiment we'd replaced in Northern Ireland. I hated it – *really* hated it – but there was little I could do.

The fact that I'd hurt a couple of primary-school bullies badly enough that they decided it wasn't worth tormenting me any more had made my life better, but it didn't mean that I stopped encountering racism. How could it?

This was the time of the National Front. They were everywhere. It could sometimes feel as if they were constantly in your face. The high levels of unemployment at the time meant that people were looking for scapegoats; the National Front pointed them in the direction of people who looked like me. Situations can turn people into someone, something, that they're not. There were lots of marches in the Midlands, including Stoke, and you'd see their graffiti – an N linked to an F – scrawled all over the place.

But then many people were prejudiced already; they didn't need to be stirred up. After I joined the cadets I went into a shop with my brother to buy a balaclava to keep me warm. The man behind the counter said, 'Oh, I know why you want this. Are you going to be robbing places?' He was laughing – it was supposed to be a joke – but that didn't really make it any better. I was 11, so it went over my head. My brother was furious, partly because he felt helpless.

Then, when I was in my mid-teens, I fell in love for the first time. She was nice, and her mum was kind to me, but the odd thing was that she never invited me over when her dad was around. I only found out later that this was because he didn't like Black people. In fact, he'd once said something to my dad, who'd just knocked him out. I guess that didn't endear me to him either. (She'd break my heart later on; I came back from my first leave from the army, dead excited to see her, only to be told, when she answered the door with an embarrassed look on her face, that she'd moved on to somebody else.)

We didn't really discuss racism much at home, which wasn't quite the same as pretending that it didn't exist. Dad once told me, 'You're Black. You're going to have a hard time. But that can't be how you see the world. Never let yourself think that life has played you a bad hand. Be proud. Always look to better yourself.'

His view was: *Don't judge a book by its cover. Take people as you find them. Treat people with respect and they'll respect you.* These weren't empty words for him. He lived those values.

If you're a good person, he thought, then you're a good person. He had Black mates, but he had a lot more white mates, which wasn't that surprising, given where we lived. Dad really believed that if you were decent to people then you had the potential to change them. They might have been raised having prejudice of one kind or another stuffed down their throats – you could show them something different. If they don't respond, well, fine, you've lost nothing. You can just ignore them. It's their loss, not yours.

Once, when I was 18 and I'd come home on leave, I'd gone into a pub on the estate and found myself confronted by a group of grown men in their forties who a moment before had been quietly enjoying a pint, but were now standing right in front of my face, exuding a prickly kind of menace.

Suddenly I felt anxious, liked I'd stepped into a situation that was already out of my control. Then they started firing questions at me: 'What are you doing here?'

'Getting a drink.'

'Why are you standing in my place at the bar?'

'Sorry, I didn't realise.'

'What's your name? Are you a Jones?' He was spitting his questions now, barely giving me time to respond.

'I'm Melvyn Downes, Sammy Downes's boy.'

'*Ohhhhh*,' he said, his demeanour changing instantly, 'Sammy Downes. How's he doing?' He was smiling now, as if the aggression of a couple of seconds ago had never existed.

This would happen all the time.

I'd take that attitude with me wherever I went in the world. The boldness that made you feel as if there was no door you couldn't go through, and that commitment to treating people as you'd wish to be treated yourself, no matter who they were.

And, at the end of the day, I'm all for people. I love chatting with anyone, whoever they are, whatever their background. That's another part of David Stirling's ethos: classlessness. In the SAS, nobody cared what class you came from, what colour you were, what god you prayed to. The only thing that mattered was that you were good enough to do the job. Everyone was given the same respect.

That idea was true within the regiment, but it was also something we put into practice with others. Much of our work was hearts and minds. You'd be surprised how a small group of guys with the right mindset can go into a village and earn their loyalty. You get on with people. You don't always understand each other. At the beginning you might not even like each other. And yet you begin to build a rapport. You realise the stuff you have in common. Then, before you know it, you're watching a football match together. I've never wanted to be like the Americans who would just whisk through that same village in an armoured vehicle, with the only sign they'd been there the food wrappers they'd chucked out of their windows. You have to show the personal side so that your relationship with the locals is more than them watching in the street as your vehicle speeds past.

It's hard to form connections with people when you keep your distance, because it's in the gaps between what people have been told, and what they've actually experienced for themselves, that hatred and resentment can force their way through. You have to resist the temptation to generalise, or draw the wrong conclusions. Every society has its bad elements, but that doesn't mean the whole society is bad.

It's why I think it's important not to rush to judgement, and to give people a bit of leeway. When I joined the army, my race was recorded as negro. Since then, the boxes I've been asked to tick to indicate my ethnicity have changed over and over again, even though I'm, obviously, the same person.

Even I'm not always sure about the right words to use or say, so I'm never going to slam somebody for making an honest mistake. Older people, especially, have seen a lot of change. I can understand how they get confused.

Later in my career, I was in Norway doing some winter training and we met an ancient, dead posh general who lived out there. He was a nice-enough seeming guy, who still wore an old-style commando hat and was an unbelievable skier.

We were all wrapped up against the cold, so there wasn't much of our faces showing. Still, we were all introduced to him, and he went along the line, shaking our hands and exchanging a few words with each of us. When he got to me he stopped, looked into my eyes and in a friendly way asked, 'What part of Fiji are you from?'

All the lads instantly started giggling. 'Stoke-on-Trent,' I said, trying not to laugh too. I can absolutely see that there are times when questions like that can be offensive – me, my kids, we're as British as anyone. But that old general wasn't trying to belittle me, he was born in a different time with different assumptions and I can't condemn him for that.

By contrast, racism, real racism, the sort that's motivated by hatred and a desire to hurt, is a cancer. For me, it's a really serious thing to accuse somebody of being racist, because I understand what it means. And that's why I'm careful about how I use the word.

It's far better to give people the benefit of the doubt. Look beyond the careless or clumsy words and assess what their intentions are. More often than not, they're innocent rather than malicious.

What I found when I joined the military was that people like the Guards who abused me in Northern Ireland were the exception. Every regiment has its share of pricks, but I was surrounded by good blokes. I had close friends, men I knew would always have my back. I was safe when I was in my barracks. It was much more dangerous coming back home on leave.

The British Army just wasn't like the American forces, which, socially at least, were still basically segregated, even into the eighties. In 1984 I went on a military exchange called Trumpet Dance, where we stayed on Fort Lewis, a massive base outside Seattle, for two months.

I was taken aback by a few things. The base was enormous, the size of a city; we had nothing like that. We could eat as much ice cream as we wanted; it wasn't a treat reserved for special days. But while the Yanks would share a pitcher of beer between a table, the Brits would all have one *each*. The thing I really couldn't get my head round was that the Black soldiers and the white soldiers didn't hang out with each other. There were clubs for Black NCOs, and hillbilly bars for the whites. That was so different from what I was used to.

◻

There was only one thing I could do as I heard those monkey shouts: use it as a fuel. This was what I'd always done when anybody had been racist towards me. Take a negative and turn it into a positive.

It's easy to persuade yourself that the whole world is against you, to lash out, looking for somebody to blame. But eventually, if you do really think that the entire world is against you, you're going to end up crushed by that belief. You cannot spend your life feeling embattled and bitter. It's far better to grab whatever spite or malice is thrown in your direction and change it into something you can use.

Our regiment's drums started up. They clattered and banged, melding with the shouts from the ranks and ranks of mates who had crowded into this gym to support me. 'Melvyn! Melvyn! MELVYN!'

The monkey calls had died away now, or maybe I had just shut them out. It was good to know that their hatred could do nothing to touch me. I did not feel sad, or even angry. Instead, I could sense the new energy flowing through me. I walked towards the ring thinking, *I'll show you. We'll see who's boss.*

There wasn't much to the fight, to be honest. Sergeant Rogers had told me my opponent was a banger. A stocky tank of a bloke who just knocked people out. Instead of relying on power and aggression, I decided to try to use a bit more of my boxing brain. He kept on swinging at me, big sweeps that I knew would rip my head off if he caught me. So I stayed out of his reach, keeping him off with a jab every time he tried to come forward. Then, in the second round, as he tired and grew more frustrated, I went for him and put him down. My victory edged our team ahead, and we held on to our lead.

The dirtyguts didn't even stay for a beer after the contest, they just stormed off onto their coaches, ready for the long drive back to Britain.

¤

Boxing was an amazing experience. I was so proud of everything our team achieved, but it still wasn't what I'd signed up for. This thought nagged away at me. And there was other stuff that was cramping my enjoyment of being in the Staffords. One night in 1988, after we'd won the army boxing final again, this time against the Royal Green Jackets, another armoured infantry unit, we went out for a drink. One thing led to another and there was a scuffle outside our barracks with a couple of German guys. I waded in to try to break it up, though not before one of the Germans got injured.

This wasn't unusual. There was a lot of fighting, and it could get quite nasty at times. This time, though, the Royal Military Police inserted themselves into proceedings. The German also claimed that he'd had his watch stolen. Because they knew boxers had been throwing punches, and because they knew that I was the team captain, and a corporal, it was expected that I'd give up the names of the lads who'd been involved. No way was I doing that; I just played dumb: 'I don't know. I don't know. I don't know.'

By this point, a German girl who'd been with our accusers that night had come forward to say that the thing about the watch was a lie, and that her two pals had been horribly drunk. But events had already been set in motion. The army's Special Investigation Branch had identified one of the soldiers who'd been on the edge of the melee, who they knew was about to get out of uniform. They followed him back to the UK, applied a bit of pressure and sure enough he coughed up the names they were looking for.

One of the problems for me was that Major Wilkinson had returned as a senior officer in the Staffords. I wasn't his biggest fan, and he wasn't mine. Now, though, I'd given him an excuse to go after me. I got a hefty fine for failing to report the fight. There wasn't enough there for him to bust me down a couple of ranks, but I could tell he was gunning for me. I had a vision of the future, which seemed to involve bad reports from Major Wilkinson, a lot of engine grease, and an all-encompassing sense of boredom.

So when B Company's Sergeant Major Ferguson, who was another soldier I really respected, and I think had noticed how unhappy I was, asked if I wanted a temporary transfer to the Gloucester Regiment, who were about to go on a tour of Northern Ireland, which would end in 1990. I jumped at the chance.

A year later I came back to Germany a married man. My mates' eyes widened when I told them my news. '*What?*' Although, to be honest, our story wasn't that unusual. We met, she fell pregnant, and the only way she could accompany me to Germany was if we tied the knot. Neither of us really knew the other, neither of us had really been thinking about a wedding, but events had overtaken us, so here I was with a ring on my finger.

One day in 1990, not long after I'd returned, Sampson spotted me walking through the base and ushered me over. 'Corporal Downes, how come you haven't gone for the SAS?' He'd never been one for small talk. 'I would've thought you would've applied for it by now, you're the type of person who should.'

'Oh, I can't, you see.'

He looked puzzled. 'Why not?'

So I patiently explained why the fact that I was Black meant I couldn't work undercover.

He stared at me for a couple of seconds, trying to work out if he was on the wrong end of a joke, then evidently decided I was just deluded and started to laugh. 'Well, obviously you can't sit in a Belfast bar, you're clearly not freckled or ginger, but there's plenty of posts where you could do something similar. And if you *were* in Northern Ireland, you could just serve on the reactive side.'

'Yeah,' I said, suddenly feeling foolish, 'I'd never thought about that.'

He laughed again, then composed himself. 'You should go for it. You've got the right.'

I thought to myself, *Wow, if he's telling me to go for it, I'm going to go for it NOW.*

I put my paperwork in, and actually had dates confirmed for me to go on selection, and then, on 2 August 1990, Saddam Hussein's Iraq invaded the tiny Gulf state of Kuwait, and everything suddenly changed. When it became clear that Britain would send troops to the region, I withdrew my papers. There was no way I was going to let my boys go to war without me.

5
DESERT RATS

wasn't the only bloke who changed his plans when the chance to go to Iraq came up. My mate Dixie was a sergeant on a posting in Northern Ireland. As soon as it became clear that something big was happening in the Middle East, he ran back to the mainland and insisted on being part of it. Our commander didn't really know what to do with Dixie to begin with. Going AWOL wasn't exactly something he wanted to encourage. But he also said that he respected Dixie's desire to get into combat, so he found a compromise: Dixie got busted down to corporal and lost any seniority. He didn't care, he just wanted to be there.

One of my section did something similar. Andy Buckle – we called him Bucks – had been in training with me, though went off to a different unit. He got bored of that life quite soon so ran off to join the Foreign Legion, where he fought in Chad. After five years he came back, got arrested for having gone AWOL, did some time in an army prison, then went on soldiering in his own unit. He volunteered to join us for the war, and I was delighted to have him with us. A lot of my section were just kids, whereas he was a big, hairy bloke who'd seen combat and knew what he was about. Over the months to come, I really valued what he had to offer.

◻

The Staffords arrived in Saudi Arabia in August. The first few nights were spent in a vast hangar that was briefly home to hundreds and hundreds of troops. The pig pen, as it was known, was punishingly hot and it stank; we were beyond relieved when we got given orders to move on.

We headed out into the Saudi desert, pushing and pushing on, until finally we came to a halt and were told to set up camp. For the next few months the 10, later 11, men of my section would be living in our vehicle, a Warrior AFV (armoured fighting vehicle). The Warrior was a relatively recent addition to the British Army; our unit had been one of the first to be equipped and trained up with them.

It was designed to be able to transport an infantry section into battle. There were four in our platoon, each commanded by a senior corporal, who in turn answered to 7th Platoon's lieutenant, a popular young guy called Adam Brancher. The 30mm cannon and 7.62mm chain gun in the turret, above where we sat, meant that we had the firepower to defeat enemy armoured personnel carriers (APCs) and lay down enough fire to suppress enemy positions. Its armour was sufficiently thick to protect us against everything from shell splinters to armour-piercing rounds.

The idea was that there was space in the hull for seven soldiers. But, even before another man came to join us, it was dark, loud, cramped and uncomfortable. Two benches sat opposite each other. There was barely any leg room, and what little extra space existed was usually occupied by weapons and kit. The Warrior clanked and juddered when it moved, and the only reason we weren't hurled into each other's laps was that we were so tightly packed. The sole concession to anything other than functionality was the inside of the door, which we plastered with personal photographs, cartoons and other pictures that helped remind us of home, or made us smile.

I liked being in the desert. The heat was the first thing that struck me (apart from the flies, as Mr Edwards had warned me back in Bentilee). It was a drier, less oppressive heat than we'd experienced in the pig pen, but it retained the power to shock you. When the wind got up it could feel as if there was a hair dryer blowing in your face. Being hot became a constant. At once so omnipresent that it was barely worth mentioning but so powerful and relentless that it conditioned almost everything we did. We sweated when we moved, when we sat motionless in the Warrior, even when we tried to get a measure of protection from the sun by lying under the camouflage netting we hung from our vehicle to give us some shade.

Some days we'd be out on big sweeping exercises – designed to familiarise us with moving in the desert alongside other armoured units and artillery. We could be stuck in our vehicles for 12 hours at a time. There was only the bare minimum of explanation about what we were doing, and why.

At other times we'd be by our vehicles, doing maintenance, refuelling or catching up on administration, the sorts of little tasks like looking after your weapons that were an important part of being a good soldier. There were days when our little enclave was covered with clothes drying and it looked almost peaceful. We made our own entertainment, taking the piss out of each other, catching scorpions and making them fight against each other, betting about stupid stuff.

Water was scarce and had to be used carefully, but every now and then they'd bring out a bit extra for us. If we dug a big hole in the sand and then lined it with a big sheet of plastic we had been issued to protect us against chemical weapons, we could fill it up and make a bath. As section-leader I got first dibs, followed by my second in command. The newest boy got in last. But even for him it was a pleasure, because although the water might not have been sparkling clean, it was at least cold.

What we most looked forward to was the arrival, every fortnight or so, of mail from home. Before we read the letters we'd always sniff them – there was something special about how clean they were. Mail was the only thing in our lives that wasn't sticky with sweat, crawling with flies or gritted by the sand and dust that climbed into every crevice of our clothes and equipment. News from home wasn't always welcome – a lot of men got a Dear John while we were out there, which could send them spiralling down – but for me it was a lifeline: I'd left a tiny baby at home before we'd been deployed, and this was the only way I could be part of her life. I just wanted to get this job done so I could get back and see her. We'd let the lads who didn't have a partner, or whose girlfriends had chucked them while we were out here, sniff our letters or look at sexy photographs that got sent to the luckier ones. However small these things might sound now, at the time they were essential to forming the bond that grew between us.

Everyone mucked in, we shared everything, because we were living side by side in this unforgiving desert environment, without a proper toilet, with barely any home comforts. We existed in such close proximity to each other and as month followed month, I came to know the ten other men in my section extremely well: every little tick, every mannerism, every quirk of their personality. I knew who I'd be able to rely on when things went wrong; I knew who could make me laugh most. They were my boys.

That didn't mean I was soft on them. Every morning, before breakfast, while all the other soldiers were tucking into their food, we'd train for 30 solid minutes. The only man who was spared was Bucks the Legionnaire, a veteran soldier who I knew I could trust to keep himself in shape – he prepared our meal.

We were in sight of all the other troops; it sent my boys mad, but I knew we needed to stay in shape because we weren't doing anything that physical while we were in the desert. I didn't want them to lose their fitness. For me, that was part of being a good soldier. If I let them drift, become fat and slow, I wasn't doing my job. More importantly, I knew I wouldn't be sending them into battle in the best shape they could possibly be. As much as they grumbled, I think they understood this. Many of them became fitter than they would be at any other point in their lives.

We all liked our commander, Adam Brancher. He was keen and ambitious for us, but open to hearing from his NCOs. Although he was middle class, which set him a bit apart from the rest of us, he wasn't as plummy as a lot of the officers we encountered. You felt he understood a bit more about how 'other' people lived. He also didn't take himself too seriously.

Poor guy: unlike the rest of us, who soon got used to shitting in full view, he was always a bit shy about going to the improvised latrine we'd dug in the ground, so he'd wait until dusk. As soon as we saw him heading over to the pit, we'd radio to each other. 'He's going for a shit, lads.' We'd then grab handfuls of little stones and run past him as he squatted, making noises like we were planes on a bombing run. He tried to vary the time he went, but we always got him.

He could have pulled rank, I guess, though we always wore shemaghs, traditional Arab headscarves, over our faces. I think he knew that we respected him, and this stupid-sounding game helped keep our spirits high. Maybe he worried that if he didn't let us do this, we might do something *worse*.

Anyway, he also knew that between us, we must have been doing something right, because we were the best. That wasn't bragging: we won 'Champion Platoon' over and over again in the battalion. We were fitter than anyone else, better shots, our drill and discipline were better. And he and our sergeant, Jack, another mate of mine, knew that we were dead reliable, that they didn't need to supervise us in any way. So they let us get on with what we were doing.

There was a reason we were called the 'Mighty Seven'.

□

If it wasn't for the little transistor radio we'd brought with us, sometimes it would have been easy to forget what we were about to do. Everyone in the platoon had flown out there not really taking the Iraqis seriously; we thought we were just going to smash them. One of the boys I was closest to in the section was a laid-back, gangly joker called Michael Flackett, who we knew as Flacks. He was a lovely lad who was still in his teens, which sometimes showed, even though he was also the sort of decent soldier you knew you could always rely on. He'd take the mickey even as he was doing whatever task you'd asked him to complete to the best of his ability.

Flacks was one of the most excited at that stage. I remember him saying to me: 'I can't wait for this war. I'm going to get a medal.' I wasn't quite as gung ho; my view was 'Screw the medals, let's just get the job done.' When I said that, Flacks would giggle, like it was *me* saying the stupid thing.

He wasn't alone in feeling that way, but before long, everything changed.

One of the frequencies we tuned into was an Iraqi propaganda station. At various points during the day, a calm, measured voice speaking accented English burst out of the speakers, warning us: *British soldiers, why are you doing this? This is going to be the mother of all battles. You're never going to see your family again. Do you realise that we're the fourth biggest army in the world? We have the strongest defensive positions, we are battle-hardened after our glorious war with Iran. Do you think we are going to let you take Muslim territory? We are all martyrs. We will die first.*

We thought to ourselves, *Wow, they are crazy.* There was something frightening and at the same time thrilling about these gruesome warnings. We became addicted to listening. And some of what they said was true. We'd been briefed about the size of their army, about how well dug-in they were. We were told that we'd likely be coming up against the Republican Guard, their elite soldiers. At around the same time, we'd been warned about their deep stocks of chemical weapons.

The more briefings we received, the more photographs we were shown, the more obvious it seemed that they were a professional outfit. We weren't going to be facing a horde of ragged convicts. I thought about the picture of my wife and newborn daughter I'd stuck to the inside of the door of our vehicle.

A few weeks after the broadcasts, Scud missiles started to fly over Saudi Arabia, each heralded by a piercing alarm. It was horribly hot as it was, but each alarm meant that for hours at a time we'd have to entomb ourselves in our nuclear-chemical suits, which were made from a charcoal-based material that we were told would protect us from whatever might be dropped on our heads. Maybe this was true, but it was so hot inside them, as well as the rubber gloves and boots we had on our hands and feet, that you felt close to expiring. Sweat would cascade down your back, and you'd be drawing in old, stale air through your respirator.

Suddenly, everything felt that bit more serious. Something else changed, too.

More and more ammunition arrived. Our training grew ever more intense. It was all live-fire now, practising the choreography of working in close proximity with tanks rushing past you: how to move and how to keep in touch with each other. This was the kind of work you did when you were about to be sent into battle.

◻

We moved again shortly after Christmas 1990, closer to the border with Iraq. That was when I knew it was definitely going to happen. Our vehicles were dug in this time, deep, and so far away from the neighbouring platoons that we couldn't see them any more.

Fortunately, we were able to make ourselves a little more comfortable, at least temporarily, when we conducted a reconnaissance patrol near an American unit. As we passed by we realised they were all asleep. It felt rude *not* to take advantage of the opportunity, so we pinched a couple of parka coats (just like the Mods used to wear, but in this context something to keep us warm when the temperatures dropped at night) and some of their rations. Just before we left, we wrote on the side of their tank: 'You've been visited by the Mighty Seven Platoon.' Nothing was ever said to us.

Gradually, the tempo of the attacks from our side began to rise. Each night we'd see the flashes above the Iraqi positions on our horizon. More and more ammunition arrived for us, along with medical supplies and other equipment. There was a quick discussion about whether we had enough body bags, before we were briefed that if anyone was killed, they were to be buried in the desert. We just had to log their grave's coordinates and move on. Even now, over three decades on, I can feel goose pimples spreading along my arms at the thought of it.

And something was nagging away at me. Because not long after we moved nearer the front, I lost my lucky spoon. This was a red plastic baby spoon that had been belonged to my daughter which I used to eat from the communal pot of rations we made for each meal. I hated that sense of breaking one of the thin threads that connected me to my kid, but I also couldn't help seeing it as a bad omen.

It's hard not to be superstitious when you know you're about to go into battle. Once it was clear it was going down, a lot of the lads started to write their final letters, to be given to their loved ones if anything happened to them. I never did – in fact, if anyone asked my advice, I always tried to discourage them. For me, doing that was like signing your own death warrant. I'd carry on *not* writing final letters right through my career, even ahead of the most dangerous, secret operations while I was in the SAS.

There'd always be a moment on those missions – after we'd been briefed that there was a good chance of taking casualties, maybe as we were in the helicopter transporting us to the target, and I was looking around at the other men sitting within touching distance of me – when I'd think to myself, *It's not going to be me.* Then I'd look around at their tense faces, and wonder, *Is it going to be you? Are you going to get it? I'm going to be first out of the door but I know it's not going to be me. Is death waiting in this tight space, ready to take one of us?* I wasn't the only one doing this.

It was always important to me to have that positive attitude where you convince yourself that you are coming back, no matter what. The loss of the spoon chipped away at that confidence at precisely the moment I needed it most.

This was the time when we got rid of anything we no longer needed. No more camouflage nets. Our sleeping bags were

122

moved from the inside of the vehicle and strapped on its outside alongside our water supplies. If they got shot up, or fell off, that was tough. Even spare uniforms had to be left behind; we just about managed to find room for two sets between the 11 of us. A big bowl would have to serve as a bathtub for us all.

Their place was taken by radio equipment and batteries, and, most of all, ammunition. Boxes and boxes of bullets, grenades and the huge shells that fed the cannon in the turret above.

We each carried our own weapons, as well as some survival kit and our water bottles.

The only personal item I allowed my men to keep was a small ammunition box in which they could store letters from home, or other mementos with personal significance.

It was weird: the inside of the Warrior suddenly felt unfamiliar. It had been our home for a long time, now it felt like the place where one or more of us might die.

There was a new seriousness to everything we did. There were fewer jokes, and people's faces began to show little signs of strain. I tried to respond to this shift in atmosphere by doing what I could to build their confidence and persuade them that everything was going to be all right. I'd remind them of how much they'd trained, of how good they were. I'd also point out that whoever we were going to be facing had been under sustained bombardment for weeks: 'There's not going to be anything left.'

That wasn't the same as feeling sorry for the Iraqis who'd been on the wrong end of that battering. They'd invaded Kuwait, after all. Though I wasn't particularly bothered about what did or didn't happen to a country I hadn't heard of until a few months ago, I was a soldier serving the United Kingdom: I was here to do whatever my country needed me to do. And deep down, even with all of the anxiety and fear, I was excited.

◻

On 24 February 1991, the attack we had been waiting so long for finally began. In the late afternoon, as the light began to fade from the sky, we heard the gigantic, terrifying whoosh of multi-launch rockets as they streamed over our heads to smash into the still-distant Iraqi positions.

We felt each explosion rock our Warrior as we waited for the order to go forward. It felt a little like being in the middle of a fearsome storm. There would be a high-pitched whine then the lightning-flash of the missile streaking across the sky, followed by the thundering rumble and crash of its detonation. On and on it went. I tried to imagine what it would be like to be on the other end of that onslaught.

I could just about make out Flacks's face in the gloom and heat of the vehicle; I knew that he didn't want to get out. I grinned. 'Do you still want that medal?'

'No,' he said, his eyes wide, 'fuck this.'

Halfway through the barrage of rockets another sharper, closer crack cut through the rumbling. I poked my head out of the top of our vehicle. A little way from where we had parked I could see men gathering around a slumped body. The whole scene was lit by our headlights, distorting shadows. As I clambered down to see what had happened, someone shouted across to me that Shaun Taylor had been shot; it had been an accident, his best mate hadn't realised his weapon's safety catch was off and he pulled the trigger by mistake. It was just a bit of cosmically bad luck that Taylor happened to be standing in the bullet's path. Once it was clear that others had the situation in hand, I returned to the Warrior. I was greeted with anxious questions as soon as I was back in the hold: 'What's going on, Mel?'

I told them as much as I knew. 'It was Shaun, a negligent discharge. Be fucking careful, lads.' There wasn't much time to think about or process the incident. A helicopter had landed to take him to a hospital, so it looked as if he was going to be OK; there was nothing for us to do.

My mind turned to everything that lay ahead of us. I wanted to have a picture of exactly where the other vehicles in our unit were in relation to us. My mind raced through different potential issues or challenges. How many trenches were we likely to encounter? Did we have enough grenades? Do we need an extra anti-tank weapon? Different tactics and drills came and went through my brain as any thoughts of what had happened to Shaun receded.

More than that, though, I knew that it was up to me to be an example to the boys sitting in this cramped metal box. I was only 26, but I was still older than most of them. I looked around and thought, *They better all follow me.* By rights I was supposed to leap out last. That didn't feel right to me. I felt I should be first. And yet I wanted to make sure that they followed me through the door, so I'd told them that I'd shoot anyone who stayed back in the hull. I wondered if any of them were thinking of this half-joke, half-threat now. Their faces were taut with nerves. I could see the acne that still clung to a couple of their foreheads, and the redness of cheeks that were still getting used to being shaved every day. 'Get a bit more camouflage cream on,' I told them, offering them my tube. I reckoned a simple task like this might steady them. There was another thump as rockets exploded somewhere ahead of us. The Warrior shuddered. I tried to smile and look confident, then raised my voice so it could be heard over the din outside: 'We'll be OK, lads, we'll be OK. No matter how loud and unpleasant it is here, think what it's like on the other side, because they've been getting it for ages. There aren't going to be many of them left.'

I went silent for a bit, listening to the steady stream of information coming through my headphones from the vehicle commander. There was nothing dramatic, just updates about our current status, but I needed to pay attention.

Then, not long afterwards, the order to move came through. It wasn't a dramatic moment: there were no trumpets playing, or men screaming, simply a calm voice telling us it was time to get going. My driver's voice crackled into my ears, 'OK. Vehicle's rolling,' then there was the grinding noise of our Warrior easing itself into a steady crawl forward.

I climbed up to the turret to look around us. I could see tanks nearby setting off. The night air was filled with the smell of diesel fumes cut through with the desert's own distinct tang. I took the scene in for a moment, then clambered back down so that I could take my place at the back of the vehicle, by the door.

This is it, I thought. *This is it.*

For a few minutes we crunched our way over undulating sand dunes. I knew that our driver was taking as much care as he could, but we were still being tossed around as the Warrior negotiated the terrain beneath its tracks. Once upon a time, it had been possible to see into the fuel container through a pane of frosted plastic. They had to black it out because people were getting seasick watching the diesel slop up and down. Occasionally, one of us would be thrown against his neighbour. There would be a mumbled apology, then silence again.

That was when I noticed the smell. It ran beneath the hot sweaty stench we had all become accustomed to. For a moment I couldn't work out what it was, then I realised: it was fear leaching out of our bodies.

I could see anxiety written on the white knuckles gripping weapons, the young kid whose knee juddered up and down constantly, the sweat running in rivulets down camouflaged faces. I started saying stupid things, like asking anyone if they fancied a McDonald's. Nobody replied – I'm not even sure if they'd heard me. Instead I smiled, hoping that if I could project a bit of calmness, it might spread to the others.

After that, we were all deadly quiet. Nobody spoke. I think we all went into ourselves. Minutes went by as we continued to churn through the night. Steadily, new noises were added to the cacophony outside. I could hear the boom of the Challenger tanks around us unleashing their 120mm shells at targets that were coming ever closer. A little while later, there was a cluster of even nearer explosions somewhere, perhaps a kilometre to our left. My radio burst into life again, 'A Company in contact.' I knew the plan was for them to attack a particular position. They were making history: the first armoured infantry attack by British soldiers since the Second World War. There was still noise everywhere. I tried to locate each of them and see if they matched the order of battle as I understood it, but there was too much going on too fast, so I gave up.

And then, suddenly, we stopped. I clambered up out of the turret to get a better view of our situation. Above, a few stars glittered in the black sky above, but the light they shone was insignificant compared to the bright glare of the explosions I could see at almost every point on the horizon. I took a deep breath of the cool night air, which was now filled with the carbine stench of weapons, then jumped down to see what was going on. In truth there was nothing for us to do. Any Iraqi that was still alive had his hands thrust over his head. The dead lay scattered in grotesque positions in the sand around me. Many had had limbs or parts of their torso blown off.

There was time for the boys to step outside for a quick piss, and then we were on the move again. This pattern repeated through the night and into the following day, all conducted in a permanent semi-darkness from all the smoke, exploding munitions and burning oilfields. It was an eerie, mad sight. We'd lurch off, trundle along for a bit, then stop, waiting for our next set of orders. Sometimes you'd be told to assault a position and find nothing there. Or you'd see a vehicle coming towards you suddenly disappear because it had fallen into a bunker.

There were more prisoners, more corpses, but that first night we saw nobody who had any fight left in them. The worst were the times when we'd come across a body far away from any defensive position or road. We guessed they must have been

128

so bewildered, or frightened, that they'd tried to walk away to what they hoped might be a safer place. Occasionally we'd pass the burnt-out carcass of an Iraqi tank – some had been dug in and used like artillery, others had been caught in the open. It was clear that none of them had stood much chance against their equivalents on our side. At some point in the course of that long night I remember watching a static Iraqi tank, an old Russian T-64, hit once, then twice, by two separate British Challengers. Its turret exploded, spinning into the sky in a blaze of fire and smoke.

Exhaustion mounted in all of us. We had been on the move for almost 36 hours and were now too tired even to be frightened, but few of us slept. We never knew how long we'd be stopping for, so although I tried to arrange it so that each time we halted a few of us kept watch while the others had a chance to rest, in practice nobody did much beyond doze lightly. For a handful of seconds you'd feel your eyelids shut and your mind would begin to drift, woozily, towards sleep, then another boom from somewhere outside the Warrior would wrench you back to full consciousness and you'd come to with a jolt. We had all lost our appetite. Instead we fuelled ourselves by eating snacks mechanically, and did what we could to replace the liquid we'd sweated out by drinking gallons of water.

Day, when it had come, was barely lighter than the night had been. Greasy black towers of smoke had drifted across from the burning Kuwaiti oilfields, blotting out the sun that had tormented us since we'd arrived. Somehow, though, this didn't come as a relief. A series of small sandstorms cut out the weak rays of light that had managed to break through the oil fumes. It was hard to make out even the closest vehicles; the only sign of their existence came in the form of the red glow from their rear lights.

We stopped again, long enough for us all to leave the Warrior. Normally we welcomed the chance to escape, but now we felt disorientated. It was impossible to get your bearings. Sound travelled strangely and perspective had disappeared. The weirdness of it all was magnified by exhaustion and the adrenaline that had become a constant presence in our bodies. I had never been so keyed-up for so long.

The second night passed in a similar fashion to the first. A series of stops and starts. We'd head off, then arrive to find nothing to do except help direct scruffy, wide-eyed Iraqis back beyond our lines, where they could be processed properly. There was something incredibly unsettling about the way they sometimes emerged from within a sandstorm. The dust that coated them and the gauntness that had come from weeks of suffering a hellish bombardment made them look like desert ghosts.

One man, a youngish guy in jeans, surprised us. As he was being searched he started speaking in a perfect Boston accent – the way he talked about 'cawfee', when we offered him a hot drink, was a giveaway. My first instinct was that he was an American Marine who'd got lost.

'Are you American?'

'Yeah,' he said, seeming baffled that I'd even needed to ask. 'What the fuck?'

'I'm American, but my family is Iraqi. We were visiting them when all of this started. They wouldn't let us leave, then they made me enlist. They gave me an AK-47, a water bottle, a gas mask and a green top, though nothing to wear on my bottom, hence my jeans. Then they told me to go and stand in a trench. I just want to surrender.'

The appearance of this poor soul who had found himself on the front line by accident added to the strangeness of our experience. At least, I thought, we'd signed up for this war.

6
THE MIGHTY SEVEN

I joined a junior leaders' course when I was 16. That doesn't make you a leader. And nor do the 44 weeks officers spend at Sandhurst. I've seen a lot of lieutenants, captains and majors come in who just did not compare as leaders with the soldiers on the ground. Most companies are run by the normal guys.

A leader is supposed to lead, not just manage. If you're in charge of a platoon, or even a company, of course there will be times when you have to take a step back, but you've also got to be there at the front, setting an example. You don't have to be the best at everything – nobody expects that – but if you aren't willing to put your head above the parapet, what's the point?

By the time the First Gulf War came around I was a senior corporal. I took that responsibility seriously, and in order to be the best leader I could be, I tried to mirror the people I'd respected in the past – the blokes who had inspired me, who I'd responded to.

In any given unit of the regular army, maybe 20 per cent of people are like me: super-keen, self-motivated. Another 20 per cent will be the opposite – just there, trying to keep their heads down and have an easy life until they can collect their pension. The rest, the 60 per cent, go where they are led. So much depends on the officers and NCOs, the standards they set, the sort of things they ask of the people they command.

The ones I liked and respected were those who actually led from the front, who showed they had integrity. They didn't just say, they *did*. If they made you a promise, they kept it. They weren't just looking out for themselves. Sampson, the former SAS officer, was a good example of that.

He helped expand my sense of what I was capable of. He demanded the best from us, but only because he believed that we had potential. Although there were some who wanted to get out of his company because they thought it was too hard, most of us were proud to be part of it. We all looked up to him, all wanted to be like him. That's the sort of leader I wanted to be.

I'd never claim to have been a perfect leader, certainly by today's standards. But I always kept a sense of humour, I'd have a laugh with my men, and there were certain things I'd turn a blind eye to. I was never going to get too hot under the collar about a good soldier coming in a bit late after a few drinks. After all, I'd done that in the past.

And yet I was also very clear where my boundaries were; there were certain standards I demanded. I expected them to look after their kit. I wouldn't abide anybody falling asleep on guard duty. When I was a sergeant, I'd expect my platoon to do PT on Wednesdays when their peers were having free time. We were getting ready for war, after all.

If someone refused to run, I'd kick them up the backside to get 'em going. Perhaps that made me a bit autocratic, I don't know.

Again, that came from Major Sampson. The bullshit wasn't important to him. What he cared about was whether you could shoot, move and communicate. That's why his training was as intense as he could make it – because he wanted to prepare us for the real thing. I loved that: you train as hard as you can, so that when it comes to actual combat, it feels easy.

Now, on the third day of the ground assault, I was going into battle for the first time in my life. I'd be leading men. So much responsibility was in my hands: if I made the wrong decision, if I went the wrong way, failed to spot a threat, or fucked up in the thousand other big and small ways it's possible to fuck up, I knew I could get people killed. I was determined to do everything I could to get my boys through safely.

ɑ

Earlier in the afternoon, our commander had taken the opportunity presented by another short pause to collect his platoon leaders together to brief them. They then dispersed among their men to let us know what was expected of us. Our target was a little way ahead, in a position that was supposed to be only lightly defended – the thick smoke from the burning oil wells meant we didn't have the intelligence we could usually expect from the air. So, unlike the previous night's attack, we'd be advancing without the tanks, who would be going off to the flanks. The thinking was that the firepower of our Warriors should be sufficient to suppress any opposition we might face.

The position itself consisted of a big berm in the sand – an eight-to-ten-foot wall that had been thrown up by Iraqi engineers. It was believed that it had been bombarded already, though again nobody could be certain.

As we approached, I could see a line of tiny figures swarming up onto the top of the berm. It wasn't immediately obvious in the failing late-afternoon light whether they were coming to greet us or attack us.

While 7th Platoon moved out on the right-hand side, 9th Platoon went to the left, with the company commanders' vehicle in the rear and 8th Platoon in rear reserve. There were 13 vehicles in all. We all strained to make out what sort of threat, if any, these men posed. Then, when we were about 800 metres away, we heard from our commander again: 'I can see weapons.' He was right; they were brandishing small arms. They didn't look like men coming to surrender.

'Fire above their heads with your chain guns and cannon.'

Overhead, our weapons opened up. As the machine-gun started chattering we could see tracer arcing over to the enemy position as heavy metal rounds clinked down, some tumbling back inside the Warrior, others clattering down its exterior. Alongside this the 30mm cannon starting pumping out its explosive rounds in the same direction. *Boom, boom, boom.* We'd used live rounds plenty of times, but always with ear defenders. Now we were exposed to the shockingly loud sound of automatic weapons firing just a few centimetres away,

We were taking fire too. I could hear it pinging harmlessly into our vehicle's tough hide. What was strange was that the volume of incoming didn't match the numbers we'd seen on the ridge. It was only later that we began to understand why they had fought back so raggedly. Before we had attacked, their lines had been saturated with propaganda aimed at persuading them to surrender. The leaflets had instructed them to do so with their weapons held up in the air. The problem was that nobody had explained this to us. So when they marched forward, holding the weapons as they'd been told to, and were met by a hail of tracer, they were understandably confused. Some fought back, while others sought refuge in their trenches.

For the moment, though, the confusion persisted. While a good number were clearly trying to give themselves up, a substantial minority seemed to want to hold out. The sand that the hot desert wind continued to whip into our faces as well as the oily smoke that hung above like a thick black blanket only added to the uncertainty.

Ting, ting, ting, ting. Another flurry of bullets slammed into the Warrior's front. It felt as if the incoming fire was getting heavier. For a final time I lifted my head up and outside our vehicle. In the unnatural afternoon dark I could see our comrades' Warriors advancing steadily on either side of us. Tracer spat in both directions. *Ting, ting, ting, ting.* Our briefing had been wrong. There was a whole battalion here waiting for us. I imagined one of the bullets thumping into my skull. This wasn't how I wanted to go. I ducked back down and wriggled my way through the forest of camouflage-clad limbs to regain my place by the Warrior's door.

Another message from our commander: 'Advance and engage the enemy.' The APC started rolling closer and closer to the enemy position. Again I wondered whether my men would follow me out of the gate. With a sickening lurch we went over the tip of the berm and started rolling down into its interior. There were even more trenches here, filled with soldiers rattling away at us with their AK-47s.

Closer. Closer. I crouched down by the door. I wouldn't be going up top again, because I needed to be ready to go. I glanced at the photo of my wife and daughter and wondered, irrelevantly, what they were doing.

'Three hundred metres.' The driver was calmly announcing how far we had to go as the inside of the Warrior got steadily darker because the lights were being turned down to get our eyes accustomed before we leaped into the night.

Suddenly I became aware again of the sheer volume of noise: the clanking of the Warrior as it surged across the sand and over abandoned trenches; the chatter of our machine-gun and the rhythmic clattering of spent rounds; the thwomp of explosions. All of it was made more intense by the fact that, for the moment, this chaos was all unfolding out of our sight.

'Two hundred metres.'

My hand edged across to the button that would release the door. The fear that I'd sensed on the first night had returned. The men's eyes had glazed over. There was that animal smell of terror. For a moment I felt an almost overwhelming sense of responsibility for these boys. I knew that they all looked up to me. I was 26 while most of them were yet to turn 20. Before, this had not felt like a significant gap; now it did. They understood that I'd been trained for precisely moments like this, I'd been on the British Army's strenuous section commanders' battle course, which had taught me new things about tactics and navigation and tested my discipline and leadership. I had a certificate that announced that I was competent to look after men in battle. And yet none of that would mean anything if I were to fail them now.

'One hundred metres.'

Something told me that this was not a moment for fine words. Or, in fact, any words. Usually, I liked to defuse tense moments with a joke, or by smiling. Not now. I nodded to them all, trying to convey as much confidence as I could. I wanted them to know that I believed in them.

I fixed my bayonet to my rifle and indicated for the others to do the same. The seven-inch blades glinted wickedly in the vehicle's dull red light. We still only had the haziest ideas of what would be waiting for us once we jumped outside the Warrior's armoured shell.

There was the piercing scrape of metal on metal as we got hit by another burst of enemy fire. I could just make out the sweat oozing out of scared men's pores.

'Fifty metres.'

I thought to myself, *We're going, we're going, we're going.*

'Forty metres. Thirty metres. Twenty metres.'

We're going, we're going, we're going. It felt as if adrenaline was rushing through every cell in my body.

'Ten metres.'

My fingers found the button, and with a satisfying mechanical hiss it eased its way open. The last few minutes had been spent wondering frantically what would be waiting for us. Now I was about to find out.

Our Warrior was still being hit as I heaved myself out of it, my boots slamming into the soft sand. There was the almost shocking freshness of clean air after the hot, dense staleness I'd experienced inside our vehicle, then I steadied myself before darting round the right-hand side of the vehicle. The next man out mirrored me, running to the Warrior's left. One by one, each of the boys who only seconds before had been frozen in anxious silence, followed me. I felt a gust of exhilaration. They'd done it. They'd *done* it. I have almost never felt prouder, at any point in my life, than I did in that moment.

Some of that was drill. We'd practised debussing like this so many times that I think I probably could have ordered them to run straight down the throat of a machine-gun nest and they'd have done it. But it was also because of the bond we'd formed living in each others' laps for months, sharing everything, laughing with each other.

Over the next few minutes we zigzagged forward. One small team running ahead while their comrades put down covering fire, then hurling themselves to the ground and opening up with their weapons as the four men that had been protecting them sprinted five metres to the next position. It was hard to make out much of what was going on. There was still an hour before sundown, but the churned-up dust had cast a dirty brown veil over everything around us, which was occasionally torn by the tracer zipping through it. We could see no more than a couple of hundred metres ahead.

Some of the enemies' bullets kicked up sand as they slammed into the desert floor around us. It seemed impossible that none of us had been hit, and yet there was no time to wonder about our luck. My mind raced as I tried to identify enemy positions while maintaining my section's momentum.

There. I spotted a knot of enemy firing at us. 'Eleven o'clock,' I shouted. 'Watch my tracer and fire your rounds that way.' I pressed the trigger on my rifle. What made everything harder was that each Iraqi appeared to be behaving in a different way. For every man that wandered towards us, desperate to surrender, there was another hoisting an RPG (rocket-propelled grenade) onto his shoulder and trying to blow us to pieces. And they might only be metres apart. My boys showed immense discipline in restricting their fire only to those who were fighting back. That was the second thing about that day that still makes me proud, because it was unbelievably hard, demanding life-or-death decisions in seconds; it would have been so easy to panic and just hammer everything.

There was no time to do much with the dazed, terror-struck men who ran in filthy, ragged uniforms towards us to give themselves up. We pulled their weapons off them then pushed them back on to our rear echelons. They seemed only too happy to be heading to safety. There were a handful of sinister exceptions: men who collapsed in a heap just as they reached us. These unfortunate souls had had their bodies torn to pieces by shrapnel, but adrenaline had kept them moving forward, almost like zombies. Still, it was strange to find ourselves in such close proximity to the enemy, who no longer seemed like the fearsome warriors their propaganda had boasted of. Most seemed either too young or too old to be fighting a war, though I knew how much they must have been affected by our bombardment. An experience like that can break even the strongest of men.

Everything had become increasingly confused. There was still sporadic fire, and what felt like a thousand different things that all demanded my attention. A stream of orders and information came through my radio from my commanders. Alongside this I was trying to organise my guys, make sure they were in proper fire positions. I needed to tell one soldier to 'Get down, move to the right.' Then another I'd have to instruct, 'Get over to those prisoners. Get that weapon off him.'

I had to take a second to compose myself and assess the lay of the land. I looked up and saw another enemy position, about a hundred metres to my right. This was 9th Platoon's responsibility. Their Warrior ground to a halt 50 metres from where I was lying, and its passengers spilled out, just as my men had a few minutes before.

The section was commanded by a mate of mine, Andy James, and I tried to make him out. At that moment, I spotted a straggling group of Iraqis with a white flag emerge from the gloom ahead. *Good,* I thought, relieved that they weren't going to present a problem. But then another figure popped up, no more than 70 metres away. There was a puff of smoke. *Fuck, an RPG.* I watched in horror as its grenade lanced forward, hitting the surface of the sand then ricocheting up again, like a stone being skimmed on water, before it crashed into 9th Platoon's Warrior. For a few seconds the vehicle and everyone around it disappeared into a cloud of phosphorous smoke. I felt my heart stop. I was certain they'd taken the Warrior out, that when the wisps of smoke had cleared I'd see my mates' corpses sprawled alongside torn-up metal.

That's the horrible thing about combat like this: you cannot stop the clock and ask to be allowed to take a moment out to see if your friend is dead or not. There is too much happening; everything has its own terrible, relentless momentum.

There was a blurry movement to my right as another soldier from my company, a corporal called Steve Ford, thudded down beside where I was lying. From the corner of my eye I watched him load the 52-inch mortar he'd been carrying. There was a bright flash, then a vicious bang and all of a sudden I found I could hear nothing. I felt temporarily dazed and there was a hot searing sensation on my cheek. Had we been blown up like 9th Platoon? I was struggling to make sense of what just happened. I started screaming, 'What the fuck? What the fuck?' But Steve was laughing, almost uncontrollably. He'd moved as he fired the mortar and its shell had passed just centimetres from my head.

'Downey,' he said, just looking at me now. 'Are you OK?'

I shook my head slowly, more to throw off the tingling that had filled my head. 'You twat, you nearly took my fucking head off.'

Steve had been sent by his platoon commander to fire an illumination round. There was still a dazzling brightness hanging up in the sky where it had exploded. It was soon joined by others that lit up everything before us, like floodlights at a football match. I could see two oblong wooden buildings, resembling large Nissen huts, lying in the middle of the pancake-flat desert. I had no idea who had built them, or why. Perhaps they had been used by Bedouin, or local farmers. One had already been destroyed; there was almost nothing left of it. Iraqis were firing from the other, but their resistance did not last for long. Two Warriors started pummelling it with their chain guns and cannon, and two sections of our troops hurried towards them. In response, the Iraqi defenders started hurling grenades at them. These exploded without causing any damage, their force absorbed by the soft sand. God knows what they thought they were doing. Somehow, this useless attempt to defend themselves added to the surreal scene unfolding before us.

After ten minutes, the Warriors stopped. The building was now a tattered, smoking mess. It seemed inconceivable that anybody had survived that onslaught. If you'd asked me, I'd have bet my mortgage that there'd be nobody left alive. It's a good thing I didn't. A spindly, frightened-looking man climbed out of the wreckage, before hobbling forward, dragging a wounded leg behind him, his hands pointing up to the sky.

◻

That was almost the last meaningful action of the engagement. Here and there you could still see a few flashes, or bursts of fire, as individual Iraqis tried to put up a futile resistance. But we had been told to halt here and hold our position. We had no idea of what else was unfolding in the war, whether or not we were making progress. But it was good to know that we had done our job.

Fresh troops moved in to relieve us. Finally, we had time and space to catch up on everything that had happened over the past days. Some of the news was hard to take. We learned that Shaun Taylor had died of the wounds that his friend had accidentally inflicted. Just as tragically, although most of 9th Platoon had escaped injury in the explosion I'd thought had engulfed them and their vehicle, the RPG round had passed through Carl Moult's chest, killing him instantly. He was a lad from Derbyshire who was preparing for his wedding. Andy James, my mate, had tried to knock away the phosphorus that was clinging to his skin and obscuring the wound beneath. At one point he'd pulled on his hand, which wrenched the arm clean out of its socket. That was when he realised his friend was dead.

By rights Carl Moult should have been buried in the sand where he fell, but our major wasn't having that. He insisted that the body should be put into an ambulance and taken back to the rear. We appreciated that.

Although the firing had stopped, for now, there was still a seriousness about us all. The joking and banter that had been so much part of our lives – that had helped us form our bond together – had been set to one side. We didn't really talk about what we had been through, but I could tell that everyone was quietly processing their experiences in their own way. When you're that tired, you don't really have time to think about war, or what's going on, or what you've seen and heard.

You move one moment, then stop the next and do what you can to rest. Over the next few days we were continually pushing forward. We kept thinking we were about to go into action again. Right through the day and deep into the night we could hear somebody ahead of us being bombed. We didn't know who they were, but it was clear that they were taking a pounding.

And then, in the permanent dusk we had grown accustomed to over the last few days, we pulled up to the six-lane highway that ran from Basra to Baghdad. This was the route that the Iraqis took as they fled from Kuwait. Here we were met with a vision of utter carnage. There was a twisted, blackened chain of abandoned vehicles – some military, some civilian – clearly looted. They were arranged bumper to bumper, like a monstrous version of a rush-hour traffic jam, extending as far as the eye could see. Flames still flickered here and there, and there was the same stench of chemicals and munitions that we'd encountered everywhere since the assault had begun. Now, though, it was overlaid with the sickening scent of rotting bodies.

God, I thought, *the air force have had a field day here.* Orders came through that we were to stop and stay in our vehicles. I could see why: legions of anti-personnel mines, dropped by our planes, were littered among the corpses that lay everywhere around the vehicles. If you stepped on one, it probably wouldn't kill you, but you might never walk again.

We didn't know it then, but this would be our home for the next three days and nights. Darkness fell, and after an hour or two we stepped out of our Warrior to stretch our aching legs and have a piss. For the moment, we were careful not to stray very far away, and always to walk where we could see our vehi-

With my brother and mum. Life wasn't always easy when I was growing up, but we always knew we were loved and cared for.

Dressed up in some of my finest seventies gear.

Aged 16, back with my parents while on my first leave from the army. Dad was such an inspiration to me.

Mum and Dad back in the seventies.

Joining the British Army was all I'd ever wanted. As soon as I got my uniform I started to thrive, and never looked back. I started out in the Infantry Junior Leaders Battalion. After that I was so proud to be part of the Staffordshire Regiment.

South Armagh in Northern Ireland, known as Bandit Country. At that time, there was nowhere in the world more dangerous for British soldiers.

In 1986 in Germany during the Cold War. This was an exercise in digging and living in trenches.

Ahead of being posted to Germany, I was promoted to corporal. At just 20 I was in charge of the eight men in our 432 armoured personnel carrier. I really enjoyed the challenge and responsibility of leading from the front.

A return to Northern Ireland. We had been sent as peacemakers, but in some areas, it was clear that nobody wanted us there.

Fighting for our all-conquering regimental boxing team.

During the first Gulf War in 1990, waiting for the ground war to start.

The cramped interior of our Warrior APC. Somehow, they managed to find space for 11 men in there.

Selection for the SAS pushed me right to the very edge of my mental and physical capabilities. But I loved the jungle stage.

Training in the jungle with my pals. As always, fitness is key!

Range work is so important in all environments – always pursuing excellence.

With CBS News and the UN in Darfur in 2005. Working alongside journalists gave me a totally new perspective on the world.

Quality time with my family – my wife, Zoe, and my children, Amy and Sam. Being away from them was as hard as anything I ever faced.

Here they are, all grown up!

QE2 Dubai Poppy Day Ball 2022.

cle's tracks. Sand had already started to drift over the mines, making them less visible, and more dangerous.

There were constant reminders of what lay just a few feet away. I saw a little dog trot cheerfully past us, a human arm dangling from its mouth. It was still so fresh that rigor mortis hadn't set in yet. The hand moved in sync with the dog's motion, making it look as if it was waving at us. My mates and I looked at each other in the gloom. *What was this?*

We waited and waited through that night. At first light we were greeted by the full horror of what we had slept beside. It was easier to see the landmines, so I grabbed one of the men, Tadge: 'You're coming with me, we're going to have a look around.'

I edged forward through the smoking vehicles. I had never seen such destruction. When I put my hand into burnt-out cars to touch the human remains inside, skulls crumbled into charcoal dust beneath my fingers. Others had not caught fire. I remember a coach that looked almost untouched. Inside, some of the passengers sat upright, their corpses seeming to stare at me with what felt like accusatory eyes, while others had suffered gruesome injuries; the pain and terror they had felt as they met their end still etched onto what was left of their faces. The blasts had popped open the boots of the cars Iraqi soldiers had stolen from Kuwait to reveal a strange array of looted goods, including dolls and other kids' toys. Somehow this detail was the most unsettling of all.

It was hard to absorb the full scale of the bloodbath, perhaps because what lay before us was so extreme, so beyond what humans could comprehend, that it didn't feel real. The stink mounted in the heat, becoming unbearable. For every man that lay there, his intestines spilling into the sand below in a sickening heap of blue and red, there was someone who looked immaculate, almost like a waxwork.

Prisoners continued to flood through our lines. They were ragtag, scared and, with the exception of some of their NCOs and officers, seemed as if they had only recently been forced into uniform. Like so many of the prisoners we'd seen over the last days, they too appeared either too young or too old to have been sent near a front line. It made me think about how, at the end of the Second World War, the Germans had tried to fill their depleted ranks with teenage boys and grey-haired veterans. But I also knew that shellshock and hunger and defeat can make men seem decades older. I think we all began to feel sympathy for these pathetic human beings who had already suffered enough.

Finally, bulldozers arrived to shovel cadavers and vehicles alike into the ground. It felt like an unceremonious way of disposing of the remains of so many human beings. But what could anybody have done?

Not long after, while we were getting a resupply, we began to hear that the Iraqis had surrendered. At first it was just a bit of chatter that swept from company to company. We were still gearing up to push on to Baghdad, so we didn't know how much to believe. Then confirmation came from higher up.

You could almost see everyone in my section exhale. It was as if we'd been holding our breaths for months. As tragic as the deaths of Taylor and Moult had been, there was also relief that our little band of brothers had come through it unscathed. Every one of them had now proved themselves in combat, and we could begin to look forward to a return home.

Though this would not be immediate. As the clean-up of the highway progressed, we began to roam further and further afield, investigating the area around the ravaged column.

We found bunkers under the sand, made from corrugated iron and lined with sandbags. They had been hidden skilfully, which meant they had avoided being bombarded from the air. But they were spacious: at least some of the Iraqis had been waiting for us in comfort. The homes they had built below the surface had double beds and carpets. A few of them were plush, almost a bit dainty; they looked like a posh relative's living room. And almost all bore the signs of having been abandoned in a hurry. Food sat untouched on plates; equipment and a few valuables lay strewn on the floor.

In one of them we found a safe. It was imposing in size and, once we managed to pick it up, seemed intriguingly heavy. After a fair amount of effort we opened it, and for a few seconds I think all of our jaws went slack. We stared at what was inside in disbelief. There were stacks and stacks of Iraqi banknotes: an almost uncountable quantity, gleaming with promise. We grabbed huge handfuls of the money. They were bright, clean and emblazoned with pictures of Saddam Hussein and Arabic script which we couldn't understand. But that didn't matter. The meaning of what we had discovered seemed clear.

Like almost everyone else in our unit, we were working-class lads from humble backgrounds. Nobody joins the British Army to get rich, and nothing about our careers had ever threatened to change this. Until now. We started to discuss what we would do with our new wealth. Our fantasies became more and more elaborate, and began to feel more and more real. The Mighty Seven had become the Moneyed Seven. Except, of course, that we hadn't. As someone very quickly pointed out, the currency was worthless. What we held in our hands was essentially just elaborately decorated wrapping paper.

This wasn't the only bounty though. We loaded up on weapons that we either found abandoned in bunkers or took from Iraqi prisoners. The lads took all sorts, even grenades. I had a couple of AK-47s and a pistol. In theory we weren't supposed to take them back with us, as nobody wanted a load of unlicensed, untraceable automatic weapons flooding into Britain, but we felt as if we had earned these trophies. And anyway, we didn't plan on letting them go.

So although we were warned that every vehicle that went back would be checked for contraband material, we also knew that there was no way that anybody was going to search thousands of tanks, APCs and Warriors. Our Warrior went back stuffed with looted gear, mostly hidden underneath the seats. As soon as it got back to the port, it was put into a padlocked container, and then we picked it up once we were all back in our base in Fallingbostel, Germany. The vehicles were stored in sheds far away from anywhere the big bosses might visit.

Like most people I took mine home, where they sat unused: physical mementos to complement the memories. But there were a couple of exceptions. Not very long after our return, there was a mysterious spate of robberies near the base. Two armed men wearing gas masks were driving up in a red VW Golf to the little *Imbiss* stands that sold snacks and demanding money at gunpoint. That said, the mystery didn't last. The Golf was tracked to our garrison, because they were just turning out of the gates onto the main road into town – they hadn't put much effort into covering their tracks, I'm not sure it even occurred to them – and it was quickly discovered that the culprits were two lads in my company.

I hadn't been aware of this crime wave. The first I heard of it was when I was told that two privates – a cheeky little lad in my platoon and another bloke who I knew from Bentilee – had been arrested. It was one of those slightly surreal exchanges.

'What's he been arrested for?'

'Armed robbery.'

'*What?!?!?!?* You are *joking* me.'

A couple of days later I went to see the bloke from my platoon in the camp nick. 'What have you done, mate?'

'Well,' he said, looking a bit sheepish. 'We just wanted some money. We thought it'd be a good idea. We just put our respirators on, pointed our guns at the guy and told him to give us some cash. It worked out well so we decided to do it again.'

They started doing the same in a few other small towns in a 90-mile radius of our base. This squaddie Bonnie and Clyde didn't make that much money, partly because there wasn't much to be stolen from men and women selling hotdogs, but also because not every hold-up was a success.

'One place we went,' my mate said, 'we put our weapons up, shouted, "Give us your money!" and he started looking under the counter. We thought he was going to bring a lot of money up. But he whipped out a pistol.'

'What did you do.'

'I shit myself and we ran off.'

'Would you ever have fired your weapon?'

'I would never have used it. We just wanted to scare 'em.'

They got off pretty lightly in the end, maybe because they were seen as being young and dizzy-headed rather than a menace to society. I think they both served six months in a military prison then got kicked out. I'm still in touch with them, through social media, and they're still the same, still living in Bentilee. Sometimes it's reassuring when things don't change too much.

After this incident, our company sergeant major announced that there would be an amnesty for anyone who dumped any Iraqi weapons they'd brought back in a bin bag he left in one of the accommodation blocks. Like the rest of my mates, I dutifully dropped my trophies off before the deadline elapsed.

□

The last stretch of our time in the Middle East was spent in another camp elsewhere in the desert. The war now felt definitively over. We had tents to sleep in. For the first time in six months we got the chance to visit an actual toilet, and to complete our business in privacy rather than shitting into a hole in the desert watched by anybody who happened to be passing by. Even better, we could wash properly, without having to use water that might already have slopped over the bodies of several other blokes. We had clean uniforms and several weeks of mail that had got backed up. These might sound like tiny things, but they felt amazing.

We were all given a few weeks off when we returned. I was determined that I would put myself forward for SAS selection again, but my bosses insisted I should go on my sergeants' course. I got my extra stripe, and was all set to put my papers in, when I was told that we were being sent on an emergency tour of Northern Ireland. It was the same group of men, and Lieutenant Brancher was still in charge. *OK*, I thought, *I've been through the Gulf with them all, these are my boys, I can't go away now. I'm a sergeant.* However, finally, in late 1993, I got to do the thing I had been dreaming about for years.

7

LIFE IS NOT A REHEARSAL

The wooden cabin was packed. There were blokes sitting silently on bunks that were crammed into every corner, with our kit and uniform taking up whatever space was left. It was bitterly cold – the coldest winter anybody could remember – and filled with the stink made by men living at close quarters. Here I was then, at last.

Selection.

In some ways, it was like being a teenage recruit all over again. There was that same sense of adventure coupled with the overwhelming barrage of new information. I'd been an expert for so long I'd forgotten how disorientating it can be to be a novice.

And, just like my first day at the junior leaders' course, when I'd found myself surrounded by boys speaking with completely different accents, there were people here from all over the military. The biggest contingent seemed to be from the Paras. There were a lot of lads there sporting red berets. Another biggish group were wearing the Royal Marines' green berets – this was the first year that selection for SAS and SBS (Special Boat Service) were combined.

You could see them massing together. Even if they'd not really known each other when they were back in their usual units, they sought each other out in this new, unfamiliar environment.

Occasionally you'd catch them shooting a dismissive glance at the rest of us, and hear barely muffled references to 'craphats', which is what they called soldiers drawn from the regular army. I always felt as if they were a bit brainwashed to look down on us, irrespective of how hard our own training had been, and the fact that people like me had actually fought in the Gulf.

A lot of them were big, the kind whose shoulders brushed against the sides of a doorframe when they walked into a room. And even the smaller ones were physically impressive. I thought to myself, *God almighty; some of these could walk with a house on their back all day.* I wasn't being coy or anything, it was just a fact that they were stronger and fitter than me. They didn't look like the sort of blokes who'd be bothered by carrying heavy weights over long distances.

I began to feel a prickle of doubt. I looked around the bare, chilly room and thought, *Do I really belong here?* How was I going to cope? How could I expect to get through when I was up against these unbelievable specimens?

Later on, as I tried to get myself comfortable in my bottom bunk, I got another fright. The man sleeping above me was an officer, and one of his mates, another officer, came over to speak to him. They launched into a long conversation, each speaking in cut-glass, educated accents. It was all 'What university were you at again, Charles?' and 'Did you know Piers at Sandhurst?'

I couldn't always follow the drift of what they were saying. They used words I wasn't familiar with, and kept mentioning people and places I'd never heard of. I managed to work out that they had both served in the Intelligence Corps. Still, I was left feeling stupid and unsure of myself. They both possessed that unshakeable sense of confidence shared by lots of people from their background. Posh twats, but posh twats who seemed so much more switched on and worldly than me. *What had I let myself in for? Why did I ever think that someone like me could even pretend to have a place on a course like this?*

Being by myself made it easier to succumb to these thoughts. Even outside the big blocks of Paras and Marines, guys from other units, like the Green Jackets or the Cheshire Regiment, had formed little clumps of two or three people. Whereas I was on my Jack Jones. Plus, I was the only Black man on the entire course.

Lying there I began to wonder whether I'd be better off saving myself the agony of carrying on and throwing in the towel now. Far better to leave with a bit of dignity than show myself up in front of these men who were clearly better than me. It was so easy to forget that there was a reason why I'd put myself forward. I'd excelled for years now, I was a sergeant, and people like Major Sampson had urged me to try. Instead of thinking about the moment I was given my beret, I began to imagine what it would be like to slink back to the Staffords as a failure.

◌

To be honest, I was still a bit hazy about what the SAS actually did. I knew that they were involved in secret work and that they were tasked with the army's roughest work, but not much more. The storming of the Iranian Embassy had been a sensation, and yet beyond that the regiment didn't enjoy the reputation it does now. There wasn't the same legend surrounding them, or the cottage industry of books and TV.

I guess that's how I'd been so easily persuaded that they'd have no use for a Black person like me.

But I did know that they were considered the best of the best, and that's what I wanted to be. I wanted the aura possessed by that old guy who'd run us into the ground, or Major Sampson. I wanted people to look at me and think: 'There's something about him.'

Over Christmas I'd done what I could to get myself ready. Even with the odd horror story that failed candidates from my regiment had brought back with them, I really had very little idea what I was letting myself in for, beyond that it would be hard. I was essentially going in blind. It's possible that it was better that way. If you're climbing a mountain, you're much more likely to succeed if you focus on the bit of track immediately in front of you than if you lean back, stare at the distant peak and allow yourself to be intimidated by the scale of the task. It's when you do that that you open up little gaps for negative thoughts to creep in. Suddenly you're asking yourself, *Can I do this? Am I up to it?*

At the same time, even if I'd had a better idea of the scale of the challenge ahead of me, I'd have done it anyway.

I've always had that spirit of, *Cool, let's get going.* I don't want to look back and think, *I've not seen life.* You can question yourself, but it's always, always better to try and fail rather than fail to try.

We're all going to be on this planet for a while, then we're going to die. It's no more complex than that. I don't *want* to die, though I've had enough near misses. What will be will be. So, while I stay away from doing stupid stuff, I'm fully committed to enjoying my life. I've always wanted to get the most I can out of it. If I'm going to die, I don't want to die wondering *what if ...?*

Maybe I got it from my dad, maybe it was just in my genes, but I've always enjoyed pushing myself. I take massive pleasure from doing anything, mental or physical, well. Even if it's just doing your taxes or putting up a shelf, you can say, 'I've achieved something today.' Once you've proved to yourself you can take small steps, you can start taking bigger and bigger strides. Doing that helps me thrive; it gives me energy. If you don't challenge yourself, you'll never find out what you're actually capable of. If you don't try, how will you ever know?

And it doesn't actually matter if you're not the fittest or the fastest out there, as long as you've given it everything you have. It's not about comparing yourself to other people. You're never going to be the best ever. You can't be the best version of someone else.

You can only be the best version of you.

Whenever I got too mired in anxious thoughts, I'd remind myself of all of this, and I found I could keep the self-doubt at a safe distance. I told myself it was like boxing. The worst bit was the anticipation; once I got into the ring, I'd be fine. I felt a little thrill of excitement. I just wanted to get started. Before long, that excitement had evaporated. In its place was the deepest exhaustion I have ever felt.

ロ

Each morning I'd wake, my bones aching, my muscles barely recovered from the previous day's exertions. As I swung my legs from beneath the rough blankets I'd feel as if I'd barely slept at all. Which was true. No matter how tired I was, my slumber was generally shredded by men farting, turning over in their beds, groaning from whatever pain they were suffering – everyone was in pain, all the time – getting up to have a piss, or turning the lights on so they could check their packs.

Once I was ready, I'd read the brief instructions that had been written on a board hung up on our hut's wall. They'd tell us the time we needed to be up and about, and how heavy our packs needed to be. The required weight steadily increased as we got deeper into the course. Beyond some emergency kit, waterproofs and our sleeping bags, which were all pretty light, we didn't have much actual gear to carry, so we all had to find a way of making it up. How we did that was up to us.

Some lads were pretty straightforward and just lobbed weights or stones in their bags. I used plastic sacks filled with sand that I taped up to ensure that the contents didn't spill out. It was easier to get the measurements exactly right with them, plus they would mould to your body once you'd packed them, rather than sitting in a big, uncomfortable lump.

There were checks all the time – before you started, at the checkpoints – the instructors didn't want to leave any scope for cheating. People had been known to hide stuff while they were out marching through the hills. On top of all this there were our water bottles and our weapon, which didn't have a sling to make it easy to carry.

Things began slowly. They had to make sure that everyone there was capable of using a map and compass to get from A to B. Nothing felt too challenging in these early stages, and yet even after the first night I returned to the hut and saw that one of the bunks had been vacated. After that, the demands being placed on us accelerated.

Once we'd stumbled blinking out of the brightly lit huts into the pre-dawn dark of another early morning, we'd find vehicles waiting to take us to wherever the starting point was that day. Here, we'd hop out of the wagon, be shown a grid reference and then told to repeat it to show we'd remembered it. The instructor, speaking in the flat, emotionless way we'd all become accustomed to, would say, 'Show me where you are going.' After that, we were on our own.

You'd set off into the wind and rain, pushing and pushing for nine or ten hours a day.

Bodies, even ones like ours that started the course in close to peak condition, quickly got worn down. We covered miles and miles of marshes, mud, climbs up hills and scrambles down them. We crossed streams that had been turned into icy rivers by biblical quantities of rain. Most of the time it was dark, and even during the day your eyes were constantly being stabbed by the wind and rain that also seemed to be trying to tear your map case out of your hands, or threatening to turn its contents into a soggy mess.

And there was always an urgency about everything we did, because we never knew how long we had to complete any given task. You couldn't afford to rest, or slow down, because that might have been the difference between passing and failing.

It was hard not knowing whether the terrain we encountered would be the same as what we saw on our maps, or if it would have been transformed by the weather. Alongside this I found that we were having to soak up a huge amount of knowledge. Little things like remembering that at every second you had to keep your weapon at arm's length so you knew exactly where it was at all times, and what state it was in. *Is there a bullet in the chamber? Is the safety on?* Big things like being able to calculate your average pace as you climbed hills with packs of varying weights on your back, or use the stars to help you navigate so you could avoid the time involved in constantly referring to maps and your compass. The learning we had to do was intense, and steep. We were expected to pick things up quickly. All of this would have been challenging, even at the best of times, but it was made even more so by the fact that we were always tired, cold and hungry.

¤

You weren't told when you were going to finish, so you didn't know, as you arrived wet and exhausted at a checkpoint, whether you would be given another grid reference or simply told to get into the vehicle that would take you back to the camp.

The checkpoints themselves weren't much to speak of. Often just a tiny storm-proofed tent. It could be hard to spot them, especially when it was dark or foggy, or the rain was lashing into your eyes, so you had to be exact with your navigation otherwise you risked missing them.

One of the hardest things, to begin with, was psychological. In the regular army it was easy to work out whether you were doing a good or a bad job: somebody would always tell you. Probably by shouting in your face. There was none of that here. No praise, no criticism. Nobody raised their voices to us, or smiled in encouragement. The instructors would tell us what they wanted us to do, then let us get on with it. They made it clear that they genuinely did not care whether we succeeded or failed. Everything they said or did seemed to have every speck of emotion sucked out of it.

You couldn't expect them to hail you, or lope across in your direction. When you reached them, you'd be greeted in the same flat, emotionless way. You'd give them your name and your number, they'd give you a new grid reference for you to commit to memory – we weren't allowed to write anything down – and ask you to demonstrate its location on a map. Then away you'd go, still unsure whether you'd made it to the checkpoint in time.

Some evenings you'd get to what you thought was the final checkpoint. You'd be done in, but happy at the thought of the truck that you were sure was about to pick you up. In moments like that, even the stinking damp hut that had become your home for as long as you were able to stick the course felt like a welcoming prospect.

And then they'd bring a cup of crappy chicken soup and you'd be hit by the sickening realisation that you weren't going back. You'd have to keep going for the whole night, your exhaustion mounting to the point that you'd begin to feel delirious. The new day would start with some greyish-looking scrambled egg and toast. You'd see the instructors approach you and briefly allow your hopes to rise. *Are they taking us back?* There would be a perfunctory greeting, then the shitty ritual you'd been through far too many times already. 'Here are your coordinates. Can you show me your destination on the map? OK, off you go.'

It's hard to put into words how demoralising the not-knowing was, to have no idea what was coming, or how long it would last.

And then, after everything was over, after you'd reached the final checkpoint, there was the drive back, which could sometimes last as much as a couple of hours. You'd sit there, shivering in the open back as it bumped and shuddered over the muddy tracks that threaded through the Welsh mountains. You're cramped, tired and still unsure whether you've done enough to stay on the course.

We'd all then stumble back into the camps. Each night the hut would fill with the stinking fug of soaked-through clothes drying on radiators. We each had to decide what our priorities were. Everyone was starving hungry, and everyone was desperate for the warmth of a hot shower. But you couldn't have both. If you went into the shower when you got back in, you risked finding that the cookhouse only had scraps left. If you wanted to eat well, you had to accept that you'd be washing in cold water. (The food was OK: potatoes, meat pies, chicken legs. Stuff designed to keep you going. If you were late, you had to make do with what was left. You might not have liked gammon, or cabbage, but if you wanted to fill yourself up, and we all did, you didn't have much choice.) I didn't do either, instead finding my way to the physiotherapist to get them to massage any aches in my legs as well as strapping up a calf strain I'd picked up as a result of the lopsided way that the mountains made us walk.

The extra muscle support, as well as bundles of ibuprofen, made the pain just about bearable. Pain was a constant companion for everyone on the course. It wasn't long before my toenails blackened, then fell off. This happened to lots of us. We'd get cramps, someone else would wrench their neck, or sprain their ankle. You were going through the pain barrier every day, sometimes more than once.

There was no guarantee that the physio would be able to see me straight away. Some nights I'd have to wait until ten o'clock for him to patch me up. Then you'd still have to eat, shower, sort your kit out, make sure you'd seen the instructions for the following day on the board. There wasn't much time to sleep. And even once you had got into your bed, it wasn't easy to nod off. Despite my exhaustion my mind would always be racing, and my body throbbing with pain. I never woke feeling rested.

¤

We all lived with the knowledge of how easily everything we had worked for could be derailed by a stupid accident, or a tiny moment of carelessness, or just bad luck.

One incident, a couple of weeks in, stands out. By this time our hut was beginning to empty out. Each night we'd return and there would be one or two fewer men in their beds. Eventually our numbers were so reduced that they shut down a handful of the huts and moved their population into rooms with empty beds.

It was a day in which snow and sleet had fallen almost continually since the moment, hours before dawn, we had first climbed into the wagon that took us to our starting point. At first I'd tried to brush away the thick gobbets of semi-frozen water that landed with a wet slap on my face then slid down my cheeks. I'd long since realised how futile this was. My wet-weather gear also appeared to have surrendered. Beneath the layers of my uniform, my skin was freezing and red-raw. The cold water that trickled down past my collar to the small of my back mingled with the sweat that was the result of hours of punishing exertion.

There was a rumour, because all we really had to go on were rumours, that if we were able to maintain a pace of four kilometres an hour as the crow flew on each challenge, then that would be enough to pass the course. I wasn't really willing to put all my faith into what was, at the end of the day, gossip, so I ran every part I could, moving as fast as I was able, stopping only occasionally, and for no more than a minute at a time, to drink and eat. A couple of times I found myself so hungry and weak that I actually felt dizzy. When this happened I'd cram a couple of Mars bars down my throat. I'd feel energy surging back through me 15 minutes later. *OK*, I'd say to myself, *time to pick the pace up again.*

The danger with this was that whatever momentum you managed to build up might end up acting against you if you lost your footing on one of the downward slopes. We weren't using the normal paths – at best there would be a trail used by sheep – so you could never trust the terrain. One moment you might be scrabbling on loose shingle, the next up to your waist in a marsh's frozen water. This was a risk I was willing to take because as I saw it, it was a risk I *had* to take if I was going to make it through.

I could feel exhaustion and a thousand tiny niggles building up inside me. I was developing trench foot because dry, clean socks had become a dreamed of but unobtainable luxury. I'd been running on empty since the week before, maybe longer. If I kept pushing myself, I was heading for an injury, or a breakdown. And yet that was a problem I reckoned I could defer. I had to keep going.

It had been hard going, even by the standards that had been set over the last fortnight. My morning had been spent slipping and sliding through valleys and gulleys then up onto higher ground, trying to identify landmarks that had been deformed by mist and rain, before I arrived at the foot of a mountain that I reckoned was about halfway along my route. I looked at my sleet-spattered map to make sure I was in the right place, then up to the peak above us. It was shrouded by fog, or was it clouds? *Jesus,* I thought, *I didn't realise it was so steep.* There was no way of traversing it; I'd have to go straight up. In a way, I was glad I couldn't see the summit. If I'd known the full scale of what faced me, I might have lost heart. I put one foot ahead of me on the stones at the mountain's base and felt the soles of my boots struggle to get any purchase on the icy rocks. Another step, another struggle. I looked up again, began to calculate how long I'd need to make the ascent, and immediately wished I hadn't. The top didn't seem to be any closer than when I'd started. *Ah, shit, SHIT* – for a second I was certain I was about to topple over. I was lurching about like a pig at a skating rink, and with my weapon cradled in my arms, I had no easy way of regaining my balance. I shifted my weight and regained control. There was no time to dwell on how close I had come to falling. A voice inside me kept repeating: *move, move, move.* I decided to stop trying to see too far ahead. Instead I'd focus on a stone a few metres ahead of me, and devote all my energy and focus to reaching it. Then I'd pick another, and another. Slowly, unsteadily, I crawled higher and higher, occasionally having to get onto my hands and knees in order to keep going. After 45 painful minutes, my back hot with sweat, my limbs coursing with lactic acid and screaming for a rest, every other part of me numbed by the cold, I reached the top. I tried to drag as much air into my lungs as I could, taking heaving gulps before exhaling great hot plumes into the freezing air. I realised I had been almost emptied by the effort the climb had demanded.

There was no view; thick cloud put paid to that. Below me was a sea of sodden bracken, interrupted here and there by a jagged outcrop of rocks. I slipped my pack off my aching shoulders, wincing briefly as the straps agitated newly formed blisters, and sat on it. It was the only comfortable seat for miles.

Jesus, I thought. *JESUS. That was hard.* I had no way of knowing how long I had to get to the next checkpoint, but I had to take five minutes. Try to force as much energy as I could into my body, take on more water. I sat there, my mind scrubbed almost blank by fatigue.

The five minutes I'd given myself to rest went by far too quickly. I hauled myself up again, cursing every single thing around me. *Why am I putting myself through this?* There was a stab of pain as I hoisted my pack, then, as I shifted my weight, I cursed again. My injured calf felt as if it was on fire. One more step. I moved forward to pick up my weapon, which I'd balanced carefully against a couple of rocks. As I did so, my right boot caught its butt and sent it spinning across ice and screed. I watched helplessly as it tumbled and tumbled, further and further away. Finally landing 30 metres down the sheer slope I'd struggled so hard to climb. I heard a ragged, anguished voice shout, 'You are fucking kidding,' then realised it was me.

I don't have time for this, I thought. I hated the idea that something stupid like this could end my attempt to pass selection. That I'd been beaten, not by the course, or by a body that had given up, but by my dumb, clumsy right foot. Suddenly hating everything and everyone, I scrambled down the steep, icy slope. Every step, every foothold, felt treacherous.

Finally, though, I was close enough to my weapon to be able to reach out and pick it up. This was one of those moments when time seemed to slow down. I saw my exhausted right leg stride forward. Acting with a momentum of its own that I could do nothing to stop, the boot at its end crashed into the weapon. The weapon bumped away, banging against rock and ice with a horrible series of metallic clangs. I couldn't bear to look at where it had stopped. It was 60 metres away.

My mind began to reel. I felt suddenly weak and dizzy. Was this actually happening? Then there was a hot stab of panic. Frantically I calculated how long I reckoned I had to get to the next checkpoint, and how long it would take me to retrieve the weapon. I tried to take stock of my reserves of mental and physical strength. I knew I had little of either left. And then I heard that little voice again. *Move, move, move.*

◻

Even two weeks in, there was little camaraderie. Or, to be more accurate, everyone else appeared to have someone else they knew to talk to. I was left to my own devices.

As I lay on my bunk I could hear the conversations going on around me, including a group of five blokes from a regiment down south who had their backs turned to me. They were looking at a map and speculating about the following day's route. None of us actually knew where we'd be going, but I guess it helped to pretend we had some control.

There were even more empty beds now. A few had had to leave because they'd had serious injuries, like a broken leg. Mostly, though, they'd pulled out of their own accord, what we called a voluntary withdrawal (VW). You'd get little bumps of surprise when you'd find out who had gone. '*Him?* Wow. Really?'

It had already been the hardest physical thing I'd ever done. It had sapped my strength and pushed me to my limits. And yet it was more than that. Otherwise, all the massive gym-bunnies would still have been here. It was about more than endurance, too. I'd found that I had to access some part of my psyche I don't think I knew existed until then. It was hard to explain what exactly it was, and why I had it while others who were bigger and tougher than me didn't. Whatever it was that made you want success on this course so much that you were willing to almost break your body to achieve it. It dragged you out of bed on those mornings when you huddled between your sheets listening to rain and sleet pummelling your hut's window and thought, *I cannot go out there.* It kept me moving forward, forward, forward even when I was crawling along a rockface on my hands and knees, knowing that if I stood, the wind might actually hurl me over the edge. Even when I was stumbling because I was so tired. Even though my back was a mass of sores and my feet were a red, ragged mess.

I carried on trying to take small steps. I'd focus on just getting through to the end of the day, or through the next hour, or just to the next spindly tree on the horizon. Whatever I needed at that precise moment. If you can break big tasks up into little sections, then nothing's ever too big for you to swallow. Don't try to do too much at once.

You could quit at any time. Halfway through your route. As you sat in the back of a vehicle waiting to go, cold and damp seeping deep into your bones. A couple of lads simply refused to get out of their beds. Nothing happened. Two weeks in, just getting your body to move in the morning had become a battle in its own right. There's no shame or recrimination. Nobody tries to change your mind. You go back to your regiment, rightly, with your head held high.

And the thought of quitting was always there. It sat like a devil on your shoulder. It whispered constantly into your ear, filling your mind with promises of clean sheets, hot baths, an end to the pain and exhaustion. *There's nothing stopping you.*

I was holding these thoughts at bay, but it was becoming harder and harder. Seeing other blokes VW spurred me on. You'd think, *Well, I'm still here.* And I could draw on the mindset of the council-estate kid who was desperate to prove that he was as good as anybody else, that he belonged here. My fear was that there wasn't much left in that well. How long could I keep going?

175

I swung my feet out of my bed and padded across to the group of men. 'Hi, guys,' I said. They all turned to stare at me. It was disconcerting to find five unfriendly pairs of eyes suddenly trained on me. 'Could I look at that please?' I asked, gesturing at the map they'd been studying.

There were a couple of seconds of silence, then one of them, a big man with a gringo tache and cropped black hair, just said, 'Coon,' then turned his head away. The others sniggered and began discussing the map again, as if nothing had happened.

I stood there for a few seconds, immobilised by rage. All I wanted to do was lay into them all. I know that's what my dad would have done. I imagined the satisfaction of feeling my knuckles smash into the big bloke's jaw. That would show him. That would show all of them. I couldn't let this go.

I felt my hand balling into a fist, the muscles in my arm tensing, ready to strike. I couldn't let this pass. What would that say about me? Anger roiled inside me. It surged into every part of my body. I went to take a step forward. *How fucking dare they? How fucking DARE they?* I thought about what my dad had told me. 'Never back down.' I'd been standing my ground ever since that day. Whatever the situation, no matter the odds, I'd fight back. I didn't care how much of a beating I took, I'd always made sure I left a mark, let them know they'd been in a fight. I would never back down.

And then I caught myself and stopped. My body was shaking, there was nothing in the entire world that I wanted more than to reduce that arrogant cockney's face to a bloody mess. Except there was, of course there was. If I got into a scrap, whatever the outcome, that would be the end of my chances of passing selection. I'd be booted off straight away. I forced myself to return to the itchy rough sheets of my bunk, where I lay, as they carried on giggling, occasionally stopping to cast a mocking glance in my direction.

The thought that I was letting myself and my dad down gnawed at me until I realised that I could turn the hatred and rage I felt into something positive, just as I had when I'd heard the monkey calls before that boxing match. I looked over at the gaggle of men. *There's no way in a million years I'm leaving this course before any of you. I will fucking die before I let that happen.*

Instantly I felt better. The anger at what had been said, and my regret at not having given in to the temptation to lamp the big bastard who'd said it, did not go away. They stayed inside me, simmering. But the heat they produced became energy I could use whenever my inspiration and will to carry on felt depleted. It also gave me a simple target. My overall goal remained passing selection, but remaining on the course for longer than every single one of those men offered me something closer and more immediately achievable to aim for.

Within a couple of days, I noticed that two of them were already gone. I passed one on the hills, going so slowly it was almost as if he was going backwards. I thought, *He isn't going to make it*, and pushed on, a new spring in my step.

That rage continued to spur me on as we approached test week.

Just before this, we were given 48 hours of leave, starting on the Friday night. The timing fell just right, as it meant I could go to the funeral of my mate Flacks. I'd learned about his death two weeks into the course, when I'd been able to snatch a few minutes to call my wife. She'd told me in a really off-hand way. 'That guy's killed himself.' 'What guy?' When she said his name, the room seemed to fall away. My mind filled with memories. I thought about his goofy smile, the time we gave him birthday bumps in Northern Ireland, his sudden terror as we'd gone into battle for the first time in Iraq. Though he'd got out, just like the rest. He'd stood tall when it mattered. Then I had a recollection of the odd way he used to feel his pulse as he sat in the back of our wagon. 'Flacks,' I'd say, joking. 'Are you still alive?' That's the thing – he'd been such a vivid, humorous presence. He had so much energy. It seemed impossible that he'd taken his own life. I phoned another friend, who'd been out with him the night of the suicide. 'Nothing was wrong with him.' Except that something must have been hurting inside him. Something was making life unbearable for him. I felt a surge of pain. Fucking hell, Flacks.

What made that pain sharper was that it came hard on the heels of another senseless death. Dixie, my friend who had made his own attempt at selection, had been shot by one of his men while we were on our last tour of Northern Ireland. The bloke that did it said that it was a tragic accident, but also that he was being bullied. Though that didn't square in any way with my experience of Dixie, when it went to court he was cleared of murder and given a two-year suspended sentence for manslaughter, which they did convict him of.

Both these deaths upset me deeply – Dixie and I had become platoon sergeants at around the same time, and we had got really close – but I'd tried hard to push any uncomfortable thoughts to the back of my mind, like I always did. I just wanted to keep moving forward; I didn't see what dwelling on these tragedies would achieve. Attending the funeral, standing by the edge of my friend's grave on a raw February day, seeing the people who had loved him stricken by grief, changed things a bit.

I'm aware that it might sound a little selfish to say this, but Flacks had always told me that he thought I would be a shoo-in for selection. 'Sarge, if anybody's going to get in this SAS, it'll be you.' It had been nice to hear that from Flacks, because I admired him. I couldn't go back in time to fix, or help, him. That wasn't possible now, if it ever had been. Passing selection, however, felt like something I could do in his memory. And for the memory of Dixie, too. Over the next few weeks, I'd think about them constantly. Memories of both kept forcing themselves into my mind: flashbacks, fragments of times we'd shared.

When I limped back into my hut, ready for test week, I paused, just for a second, as I entered the door. *This is for you, boys,* I thought. *I'm going to do this for you.* My desire to kick dust in the faces of my two remaining enemies had given me one incentive. Now, I had another. I had inspiration to go alongside my anger.

Which is just as well, because everything got harder for the handful of us who were still on the course. The instructors stopped giving us proper maps to help us navigate. Instead, we had to make do with sketches. The distances we had to cover got longer, and we were expected to complete them faster. It would all culminate with a challenge known as endurance. All of the candidates would have to cover well over 60 kilometres of punishing terrain in less than 24 hours, carrying more weight than we ever had on our backs before.

Endurance came and went. At its end I was still there, along with a few green and red berets, and a scattering of blokes from the regular army. We knew that our next challenge was in the jungle. Tired as I was, the thought of this excited me. One night, as we were packing our kit, I overheard another conversation in the hut. The cockney was spouting off as he usually did. 'We'll see how these twats do in the J.'

I felt the familiar niggle that I got whenever I heard his nasal voice. By this stage, it had the same effect on me as nails being scraped down a blackboard. Why was he saying that? He'd never even set foot in the jungle! This was followed by a more pleasurable thought. *I'll show that prick.*

8

SALAD CREAM

There was more soldiering in the jungle; it wasn't just about how much you could endure, they were also trying to probe how high your ceiling was. How would we perform under pressure?

You're doing navigation, you're doing big hikes, you're doing tactics, you're doing live-fire attacks. You have to learn what boiled monkey tastes like (bland), as well as how to make termite cakes (by squeezing a handful of them into something that resembles a protein ball – it's not too bad actually).

What the instructors who shadow you at all times want to understand is whether you can operate in a team, and whether your administration is good enough for the jungle environment, because if you can soldier in the jungle, you can soldier anywhere.

If they check your weapon at any time, it's got to be perfect. Your water and your pack always have to be ready. You've got to know where every single piece of your equipment is and be able to locate it in seconds. You've got to be able to operate in deeper darkness than you've ever encountered, without making a noise or leaving any trace that you've been there at all.

Everything about being in the jungle was draining. If you move, you sweat. If you stay still, you sweat. You can't sleep without something crawling over your face, or scratching you, or stinging you. You're soaking wet almost every second of every day. Your clothes get so filled with mud and salt and gravel that they end up rubbing your back sore, like carrying sandpaper under your pack. Your body becomes so clogged up that prickly heat, like relentless pins and needles, spreads across it. It gets so that you can barely breathe. You get used to waking up and finding leeches stuck to your feet, fattened on your blood. Everyone gets worms. I came out of the jungle with what we called a tracking worm living beneath my skin. The doctor had to spray it with a solution that froze it to death. I've still got the scar.

In the improvised camps you call home, everything smells of ammonia. You stink, really stink, as does everybody around you, and you end up welcoming the point when you all get so accustomed to the stench that you stop noticing it. To anybody else, you smell like warthogs. Nobody shaves, because the air is so humid that if you cut yourself your wound might not heal.

There is noise, every second of the day. Insects chirping. Animals rustling. Rain incessantly hitting thick leaves. The eerie chorus, *whoa, whoa, whoa*, that started up each day just before night fell. The jungle was full of deadfall. Trees rot, or die, and then you have branches hurtling down from hundreds of feet up. At night you can hear them crashing, crashing, crashing in the darkness. Part of being alert when you were making camp there was being aware of what might fall onto you. Sometimes this was possible, a lot of the time it wasn't.

A mate of mine got lucky when we were staying in the same place for a couple of nights. One day we came back to find that a massive tree had fallen onto the exact spot he'd strung his hammock. If it had toppled just a few hours earlier, he'd have been flattened.

Occasionally we'd use trees like this that had landed across ravines to help us cross them. It was terrifying. You didn't know if its interior had rotted, or been eaten away by animals. You had to be so careful you didn't slip. Every step you took really could have been your last.

Me? I loved it. I loved the challenge and the way it super-charged my senses. You can sniff things out over great distances, you can hear further than you ever have in your life. It even changes the way you see. When you first get there, the dense, almost primeval vegetation seems opaque, like a wall. It's so thick, so bewilderingly similar, that you can't even go for a piss by yourself, you have to take a partner. If you head off alone, you risk getting lost in seconds. After a while, you learn to look *through* it. You can spot gaps, and in them you might catch a small flash of movement, or a bright fragment of white skin.

What really thrilled me were those times when you were certain that you were entering undisturbed parts of the forest that no human being had ever visited before.

□

It was in the jungle that I saw off the big cockney guy with the tache who'd called me a coon. About two weeks after we'd got there, he walked past my bivouac, loaded up with kit on the way to the helicopter pad. I thought, *That's him going.* I gave him a little smile, he just put his head down.

My feeling of triumph didn't last long, though. Suddenly I asked myself, *Who's my target now?* Even without a target to focus on, I made it through to the last major phase: escape and evasion, as well as resistance to interrogation, which would take place back in the Welsh hills.

Nothing was harder than this. It was the ultimate expression of the instructors' desire to push you to the absolute edges of your physical and mental capabilities without actually inflicting serious injury.

We were given a couple of weeks of training to prepare for it. There was basic stuff, like how to survive off the land, or how to navigate using the stars, but they also had experts come in to talk to us. There were a couple of Americans who'd been POWs in Vietnam. Terry Waite, who'd been held hostage in Lebanon for over four years, also spoke to us. The best one, though, was a little old lady who was one of the world's leading experts on fungi.

I remember how she walked in, as dainty and proper as you like – slightly bent, grey hair, an ancient frock – and I sank back in my chair, absolutely convinced that I was going to be bored out of my mind. Instead, it was probably one of the most interesting hours of my life. She told us which mushrooms were and weren't edible, and how we could use them to ease pain and clean wounds. The thing that blew my mind was that there was a particular fungus that grew on bark and that no matter how wet the weather was, even if the tree was covered in snow, you'd be able to light it after you'd ripped it off.

Once lit, it smouldered for hours, and nothing short of a bucket of water would be able to put it out. You could run with it, or use it to keep your hands warm. Incredible.

The idea behind escape and evasion is that it's an anticipation of the sort of thing that the regiment does. The SAS often operates behind enemy lines, so its operators are much more likely to be separated from their comrades or be captured, and need to know how to evade a larger enemy force. Each of us was let loose with an old Second World War-style greatcoat and a pair of laceless boots. We were blindfolded and driven to an unknown location, where we were handed a sketch map and told that we needed to rendezvous with an 'agent' at a particular location. It was only possible to move at night; if you tried during the day you'd be guaranteed to get caught. And if you got spotted anywhere near a road or a track, you were instantly off the course.

So we had to try to navigate over marshes and hills in the dark. When we reached the checkpoint, we were given another location, a mouthful of bread and cheese, and sent on our way. This process was repeated over and over again for several days and nights.

All the time we were being hunted by more than a thousand soldiers who'd all been promised a bonus or a long weekend if they managed to get us in the bag. They were accompanied by helicopters and police dog-handlers. Even the local farmers had been told to inform our hunters if they spotted anyone suspicious on their land. Anyone who got caught was taken away, beasted for a few hours, then released again.

The evening of my second day on the run found me in a stinking ditch. I'd made a kind of tunnel for myself by pulling branches and vegetation over my body, and now I was hungry, cold and wet. I shivered uncontrollably, occasionally wriggling a little in a futile attempt to find a more comfortable, drier patch in which I could lie. The previous night I'd split up with the man I'd been paired with as we sprinted blindly in the dark, away from the hunters whose torches we'd spotted approaching us. The following hours had been spent splashing across streams to try to throw the dogs trailing me off my scent. Once I'd found this ditch, I'd laid there through a day lashed by constant rain. Was it really summer? Some people can sleep in the cold. But as soon as my feet or toes get chilly, that's game over for me. So I'd not managed more than a doze of a few minutes, despite my best attempts. My legs and arms had been ripped to shreds by thorns in the undergrowth I'd occasionally had to crawl through. The greatcoat wrapped around my shoulders was so sodden that I doubted its ability to offer any warmth at all, but nor could I contemplate abandoning my only piece of outerwear.

And then I heard high shrieking yells. The dogs were near me again. The hairs on my arm stood on end, my heart pounded. I knew this wasn't real, and yet I had worked hard to persuade myself that it was. That I was being chased, that I might be tortured or killed if I was captured. I'd figured that if I raised the stakes like that, I'd be less likely to throw in the towel when I was tired, or hungry, or cold, or fed up. The barks grew closer, accompanied by the muffled sounds of men talking. I pictured them swarming around the area, their feet bringing them closer and closer to my hideout.

A fragment of my training came back to me. If I could control my breathing, I'd be able to rein in my fear, which would mean I was less likely to give off the pungent scent that we produce when we are frightened, which the dogs would have been able to pick up.

My breathing remained calm, coming in slow, even draughts. The voices were more distinct now, I could hear the dogs panting. Damn, was this the end? I'd chosen a spot so choked with nettles and rotting mulch that I was sure that nobody would willingly stop to investigate it, but what if I'd made some stupid error that had led them to me? My mind cycled through all the possible options.

They were just metres away. Twigs snapped, grass tore. My heart started to thump, so I turned my attention to my breathing again. *Please*, I thought, *don't let me be captured*. And then the sounds grew more distant, before disappearing entirely. They were somebody else's problem now. A few minutes passed, I dared a glance through the thatch of plants. Night was falling. It was time to move.

□

One, then two, then three and four days and nights went by. It was the last day of this stage. The end was in sight, though we knew that in a sense our suffering had only just begun. If we made it through, we had countless hours in the bag waiting for us. I wasn't sure if I was ready for this. I'd never felt so feeble or alone. Once I'd seen off the last of my enemies in the jungle stage, I lost the motivation that my anger towards them had given me. I thought briefly of Dixie and Flacks. I still wanted to do this for them; I wanted to do it for *me*. But I knew that wanting something and being able to *do* something can often be very different things.

It was still dark and I walked carefully through a ragged piece of woodland. And then I thought I spotted a face leering at me through some foliage. Yes, there *was* someone. I could see a bald head surrounded by a fringe of matted hair. The man's eyes were wild, his cheeks sunken, his skin almost black with dirt, at least where it wasn't covered in grimy stubble. *What the hell?* Just as I was beginning to feel alarmed, the face broke into a crooked smile. It was Sammy! Sammy was one of the oddballs on the course, a Marine in his mid-thirties – towards the upper age limit – who was trying to get into the SBS. We'd joked that he looked like Krusty the Clown from *The Simpsons*. In a way, he still did, though only if Krusty had spent the best part of a week hiding in a filthy trench in Wales while packs of dogs hunted him. I started to giggle at the thought, then realised that I probably looked just as repellent.

We moved towards each other and crouched down to have a whispered conversation. 'Did you see the farm about five hundred metres away?' he asked.

'Yes,' I said, wondering what he'd spotted.

'We're going to have to get some food. What have you had?'

'Oh nothing, hardly anything, you know what I mean? I've found a few of the roots they told us about, not much else.'

'Let's go see what we can find at that farm.'

I could see his point; we didn't know what exactly we were going to face while we were being interrogated, but it stood to reason we'd need as much energy for it as we could muster. Even the idea of failing at this, the final hurdle, was devastating. We agreed that I'd keep watch while he went to investigate.

From my perch a hundred metres away, I saw him illuminated by an outside light that blinked on as soon as he got close. For a minute or two he scuffled around in a big bin, then rushed back with a triumphant smile on his face. *Good, he's found some food.* My mind ran away with me; maybe there was a loaf of bread, or even a couple of brown bananas. I wasn't picky.

'Look at this,' he whispered, brandishing a plastic bottle in my face. Salad cream.

I took it, sceptically, and examined the label. 'It's three months out of date. I don't want to get the shits, no way am I eating that.'

'Come on, have some!' As I shook my head, he picked up a stick and started jabbing it into the bottle, bringing it up coated with thick gobbets of the salad cream. 'This is lovely.'

◻

Sammy and I stuck together, right up to the point when we were stopped by masked men who grabbed us roughly, planted bags on our heads, and then shoved us onto the back of a truck half-filled with horse manure. As more and more candidates were picked up, they'd be hoisted onto the truck, thrown carelessly so that they landed painfully on the blokes below them.

The truck rattled, our nostrils filled with the stink of shit and the bodies of men who'd spent days living in the wild. I tried to remind myself of the instructions we'd been given about what we were allowed to reveal. Name, rank, number. We weren't supposed to say yes or no, and if we signed any piece of paper put in front of us we'd fail the course immediately. We should accept any food or drink we were offered. But we were to try to avoid upsetting them. In theory, this is all simple. In practice, when you're exhausted and disorientated and on the wrong end of the tricks of experienced interrogators, it's anything but.

I don't know how long we drove for. After a while we were bundled off and led to the interrogation centre, where our blindfolds were removed. It was dark, so I could see very little, especially while my eyes adjusted. But I could instantly feel a change in the air temperature. For the first time in a week, I was warm.

Instantly I began to feel drowsy, almost swaying on my feet. Perhaps I dozed while standing there, waiting for my turn, perhaps I didn't; I cannot be sure. I do remember being led into an even warmer office. And I remember the way that the interrogator started talking to me in a soothing Canadian accent. I tried to focus. Everything in my mind seemed fogged. He spoke slowly, or at least he seemed to; it was so hard to be confident about anything. I began to drift off. I was going deeper into sleep. It was as I was dreaming that his voice broke through into my consciousness again. '… thank you so much for telling me about your wife and kid.' I came to with a start. *Jesus, had I? No, this is a trick.* I turned to the man sitting beside him, trying to work out whether I'd really given this information away. This didn't really help, because he appeared to have turned into Mickey Mouse.

On one hand, I knew that they were doing everything they could to break my mind. I'd signed something waiving my right to sue if they deranged me permanently. On the other, I found it so hard to resist. If they break your body, you can almost always find a way back. If they break your mind you risk being lost for ever.

The interview ended and I was hauled out, bewildered and not confident that I hadn't betrayed myself. I'd learn later that an officer on the course had been persuaded to put his signature on a document. Once he'd crossed that line, he started cheerfully signing paper after paper. That was the end of him.

When we weren't being interrogated, we were forced to sit blindfolded in a stress position, cross-legged, back upright, with our hands on our heads. Occasionally a cup of water would be brought to our lips, to allow us to sip it. If at any point you slumped, or fell asleep, a guard would be on you in seconds, slapping you to bring you back up. Our bodies aren't designed to stay like this for any concerted period of time. Before long, every limb was filled with excruciating pain. Our discomfort was amplified by them flashing strobe lights at us and blasting our ears with white noise played at an ear-splitting volume. We had to piss where we sat.

Sometimes they strode over and started beating us. The worst was a guy who really seemed to enjoy it. They were supposed to be completely anonymous, but I worked out what regiment he was because during one flurry of punches my blindfold slipped and I could see his regiment's distinctive insignia on the ring on his finger. In a very small way, having this bit of knowledge helped. I felt as if I'd won a little victory.

The only relief, if you could call it that, was when you were returned to the interrogation room. I tried to make these sessions last as long as I could, because it was warm and you could sit on a proper chair. I'd feel a stab of anguish every time they took me back. Deprived of sight, my other senses sharpened. I became extremely sensitive to smell, so much so that I could tell when the guards had changed over. One guy had distinctive aftershave. Another was a smoker. Even if they weren't close, I knew exactly which one was watching us.

Their personal scents acted as a kind of clock for me. I was able to track time passing by making a mental note each time the smell in the room changed. I'd estimated they were doing four hours at a time. This helped because it stopped me feeling completely unmoored. It also gave me a way of measuring how much longer I had to endure this torture.

At some point after 7am, by my reckoning, I was brought into the interview room, where they told me to strip myself completely naked. There was a bloke I'd seen before and a new inquisitor, a good-looking blonde woman. I couldn't help but notice how tight her black top was. *Why on earth am I thinking about that?* I did what I could to focus. They made me open my legs, touch my toes, pull my butt cheeks apart. It was nasty, humiliating, though nothing I couldn't cope with.

Then the interrogation began. To begin with it was standard fare. They did a bit of good cop, bad cop, switching between threatening me and offering me hot food and a shower if I signed the piece of paper they'd slid across the table to me.

I imagined standing beneath a cascade of warming water that soothed my aching limbs and washed off the dirt that encrusted every inch of my skin. My hand twitched. *My God, it was tempting.* Everything we had been told in our briefing now seemed very distant, almost irrelevant. *It couldn't hurt, could it?* With an effort I dragged my mind back to the room and shook my head. 'No,' I said, smiling. My sense of reality still felt frayed. But I had one thing to hold on to. I knew that in July it got light at about four. I also knew that the interrogation phase usually finished at around 11am. And that would be it, I'd have done it. I was sure I'd already seen a glow of light through my blindfold and that an entire rotation had passed since then. This was the last block of four hours I needed to survive.

The woman leaned across the table. Something in her face changed, her eyes filled with malice. She pointed to my penis. 'Pull your foreskin back.' I did what I was told. 'Now pull it forward.' Again, I obeyed. She repeated the instructions. Baffled, I carried on. Then she sneered at me. 'Are you wanking over me, you disgusting nigger?'

Right, I thought, *this is the game, is it?* To be honest there was no word she could say that I hadn't heard as a kid. Her insults took a more demeaning turn. Then, somehow, as she edged that bit closer to me, and I saw her chest in my eyeline and smelled her perfume, I imagined her naked. It was just for a fleeting second, but it was enough. Blood rushed to my penis; it jerked upwards. *Oh, God.*

She noticed immediately and did her best to control her reaction. A smile flashed across a face, then after a brief struggle, she laughed. Then I did too. It was all so ridiculous. And yet it could mean failing the course. What a way to go. We'd been told we had to take it all seriously. That's why I'd played it as if it were for real. The idea that *this* might be the reason I got chucked off felt cosmically unfair. And yet, I wondered, maybe it was a weakness in me they'd managed to find. That's what they were here to do. Panic mounted in me.

As I contemplated this, she managed to master herself. 'Get that Black bastard the fuck out of here!' I was blindfolded, dragged out and thrown onto a hard concrete surface. The man was screaming obscenities into my ear. I heard the hiss of water, then felt a vicious jet of icy liquid slam into me. Someone had turned a high-pressure hose on me. Its jet was so strong that it lifted my blindfold. I was outside. It was also dark. I'd somehow convinced myself it was eight in the morning. It was clearly still the dead of the night. There were still hours to go. *God almighty, I'm not sure I can do this.* The finishing line was in sight, but I was so tired, so addled. I came closer in those moments to quitting than at any other point of the course. My miscalculation devastated me.

This is it, I thought. I saw no way I could go on. It was precisely at the moment that I felt as if I had sunk as low as I could that I heard someone being pulled past me, one of our guys, sobbing like a baby. I heard some shuffling and pushing, then sensed that whoever he was had been placed in the stress position nearby where I lay. He carried on crying in that relentless way children do. *He's in a worse state than me. I wonder who it is?*

That's when I got an unmistakeable whiff of salad cream. It could only be Sammy. I thought of his funny sad face, his clown's tuft of filthy hair. For the second time in 30 minutes I found myself giggling. Somehow, this was exactly what I needed. No matter how bad I thought I had it, it was nothing compared to what he was going through. It wasn't much, but it was enough to get me through the last stretch of the ordeal.

◻

The news that we had passed was given to us in the same flat, affectless way that all information had been delivered to us.

I looked around the cold hangar at the handful of other soldiers, including (I was pleased to see) Sammy, who'd made it. Every single one of them looked crazy. Their eyes were enormous and spaced-out. Their cheeks were hollow, their skin sallow. These defeated, wasted blokes were unrecognisable from the strong, healthy specimens who'd started the course. And yet they were the ones who had passed. I was too broken to react immediately. It was only later that I felt my spirits soar. *I've done it.* This was followed by another thought. *Dixie, Flacks, this was for you.*

9
BEAT THE CLOCK

We were given the sand-coloured berets we'd worked so hard for in front of the clock tower at the regiment's headquarters in Hereford. There were no congratulations, no pats on the back, but it was still phenomenally exciting. Part of me still couldn't believe I was here. The major conducted the ceremony in an easy, informal manner which I'd soon become used to. 'Whatever you do,' he said, 'enjoy it. Time will fly by before you know it.' He clicked his fingers. 'And for fuck's sake, beat the clock.'

At the time I didn't understand what he meant. It was only later, talking to someone else, that I found out. Anyone who died while in the service had their names put on the clock tower. If you beat the clock, you'd got out alive.

There was little interest in letting us do a victory lap; the whole focus was on us hitting the ground running. You could potentially be sent on an operation immediately after passing selection. Which is why just a few days later I found myself in a meeting with my squadron. I entered the room expecting to find a room full of well-turned-out soldiers waiting expectantly for our briefing to begin. Instead there was a handful of scruffy men, of every shape and size imaginable, sprawled across their chairs, chatting like they'd just bumped into each other in the street. Some were in civvies, others in training clothes, and even those who were wearing uniform had managed to give every item a sort of renegade quality. Most pulled on drooping cigarettes, which they held carelessly in their hands.

I already felt a bit bashful, because we'd been asked to do some parachute exercises after selection, and on one of the jumps I'd caught my foot in a rabbit hole when I landed, fracturing my right ankle. Showing up with part of my leg in plaster clearly wasn't the best impression I could have made.

Convinced that I'd walked into the wrong room, I almost turned on my heels. It was clear that everything I thought I knew about the army was going to be turned on its head.

One of them looked up at me. 'What's your name, mate?'

'Mel,' I said, not sure if this was an adequate response.

'Yeah, OK, Mel, come and sit down. Let's get on with the briefing.'

I smiled, relieved to have negotiated this hurdle, and eased myself into an empty chair.

A couple of minutes later, the sergeant major sloped in. He registered my presence and smiled. 'Mel—'

A hard-wired instinct kicked in, and I leaped up. 'Sir.'

His face rearranged itself into that of a teacher giving an unpleasant but necessary lesson. 'Never, ever, call me sir. We use first names here.'

I nodded, mutely, afraid that another stray 'sir' was about to escape my mouth.

'OK, unfortunately you seem to have broken your leg, you twat,' he paused for a second, grinning broadly. 'Never mind. Don't worry. I'm putting you straight on a medical course.'

A couple of months later, once my leg had healed, the squadron sergeant major called me over.

'Mel, how's your drill?'

'Yeah, good.' I suppressed my hard-wired impulse to call him by his rank.

'Good, you're going to be on coffin party.'

A bloke who'd been on selection a little while before me had been killed on operations. This brought home to me the other side of the coin. This is what the major had been talking about when he told us we had to try to beat the clock. More than any part of the army that I can think of, death is an unremarkable feature of anyone's existence in the SAS. There have been perhaps one or two years in its entire history that have passed without having to bury one of our comrades. I felt sad for the guy and his family, but also a renewed urgency, like somebody twitching at my reins. It made what had previously been an abstract thought into something tangible and real. *I need to be good. There is no space for fucking up here.*

The thing is, I thought I'd been good, and I *had* been good by the standards of the Staffords, but everything here was on another level. There was a huge amount of tactical information. The SAS operates in places no part of the regular army does. And when we are in the same places, we're doing totally different things, in a totally different way. I was having to re-think and re-learn so much.

Each of the squadrons had their own identity. D was known as the most formal, while B were the most chilled out – even by our standards they were super-relaxed. G Squadron had all been in the Guards, which gave them something different, while A Squadron were known internally as the 'Strange Blokes', because they were just odd, with an incomprehensible sense of humour.

I remember just absorbing the way the other blokes talked, and all the things they'd done. I did some counter-terrorism training early on and was blown away by how much everyone knew, and how the kit they had was second nature to them. I was being hammered with piles and piles of new information: almost more than I could cope with. And I thought, *Wow, I've got to catch up here.* You are only remembered for your last fuck-up.

There was never a moment when I thought that having made it through selection, I could now just sit back and chill out. We were asked to do everything to standards far higher than anything I'd ever encountered before. I was shocked at how many words a minute we had to be able to send and receive in Morse code. I went on an explosives course and came out the other side with as much technical knowledge as most industrial engineers. The medical course was unbelievable, too. As part of it I spent time in a major trauma unit, following a surgeon. The shadow hovering over this training was the worst-case scenario of being on a mission where we might need to look after a seriously injured comrade for several days and nights with the limited medical equipment we were able to carry.

I was like a sponge, though, trying to soak up every single piece of information I could. Sometimes I'd have flashbacks to all the time I'd sat, bored and unengaged, in classes at school. My teachers would never have guessed I'd be learning how to carry out minor surgery, or studying the inner workings of an oil rig. And yet, of course, just as with the basic hunting techniques and elementary rifle drills that had thrilled me as a cadet, I knew that everything I was being taught here was stuff that would be *useful* to me.

I think I always knew I'd get into the SAS. But whatever I ended up doing, I know I'd have done it to the absolute limit of my abilities, otherwise, why bother? There's an old saying. If you're going to be a private, be a *good* private. If you're going to be a gunner, be a *good* gunner. If you're on a mission and your job is to just carry the ladder, make sure that nobody has ever carried a ladder better. You're never too good to work hard or get your hands dirty. Have a bit of humility.

That ethos works whatever you're doing. Whatever your job is, turn up five minutes before it starts and push yourself to do the absolute best you can. If you're at McDonald's flipping burgers, you flip them faster and better than anybody else. Maybe if you do it well enough, you'll become a manager. Then you do everything you can to excel at that, and move on to the next stage. Build up, build up, build up. Be the best you can be.

Sometimes, when I was a kid, I'd watch my dad as he worked. He was a really skilled, deliberate bricklayer. When he built a wall, everything had to be perfect. He was willing to knock things down and start again if they were even a millimetre out, because he wanted things to be excellent. He had standards for himself that he insisted on meeting.

He wanted us to have that same attitude. He was so, so proud of me, I always knew that. But he also felt that it's always possible to improve, to find something new in yourself. I remember sitting beside him one night as we watched Muhammad Ali demolish another opponent. Dad turned to me and said, 'You can always do better. You *can* be the greatest. Work hard and you'll always do better.'

It was exciting to feel that he had that faith in me, and just as exciting to think that it was in my hands. Success isn't just a question of the gods leaning down and handing out talent to random people. I didn't get into the SAS because I was born with something magical that set me apart from others. It was about how much I was willing to put in to get through selection. Everything good that's come in my life has come because I've worked incredibly hard for it.

That was one of the reasons why I liked being in the SAS so much. David Stirling talked about the unrelenting pursuit of excellence, and that attitude was central to everything we did. You'd drill and drill and drill until you could do everything perfectly. We did that precisely because we all knew that stuff goes wrong all the time. No operation ever goes entirely to plan. There will be parachutes that haven't been packed properly because the person responsible had been on the piss the night before, equipment that malfunctions, faulty intelligence. There's so much that you can't control, because the real world is a messy, complex place. But you can work hard to ensure that you're in the best possible shape to respond to those unexpected crises, and learn whatever lessons you need to from the experience.

It's why we'd always do an after-action review as soon as a mission had finished. How could we have done it better? How can we be faster, stronger, cleverer? You never sit on your laurels. Like my dad said, you can always improve.

¤

I was learning fast, but some old habits died hard. Ahead of my first Remembrance Day parade, the sergeant major walked into the interest room, a meeting room whose walls were covered with memorabilia from the regiment's history. We'd always show it to visiting dignitaries, because it was 'interesting'. When you first go in, you're wowed by all the pistols and paintings. Before long you stop noticing them and it just becomes somewhere to get a brew and catch up. 'Gentle reminder, lads, that you're going to be on parade in front of the public, so make sure you're in your best kit. I'll be round at 10am to do an inspection. Be smart, for once.'

I started getting ready at 8am. I was the first one into the barrack block where we stored all our personal kit. To begin with I didn't really think about it; I was too busy getting my best kit out. Over the next few minutes I ironed my shirt and polished my boots to the point that they shone. At 9am I was still alone. *Where is everyone?* I carried on fiddling with my uniform, anxious to make sure that I looked perfect. Whatever their informality, I knew that Remembrance Day was important in the regiment, I didn't want to let anyone down. When 9.30 came and went without any sign of another soldier I started to worry. *Have I got the time wrong? Am I in the wrong place?*

At about 9.45 I could hear a rumble of voices in the corridor, a stampede of feet, and then the door swung open and a rowdy scrum of blokes crashed through. They looked as dishevelled as they usually did, in fact more so, because they were pulling on various items of creased uniform as they stumbled into the room's centre. Each man seemed to be engaged in a desperate attempt to locate the item of kit that would complete their ensemble. 'Anybody got any good boots I can borrow?' 'Who's got an extra poppy?' 'Where's my number two shirt?' 'I need a tie!'

After ten minutes of chaotic negotiation they were all satisfied that they were ready, and we arranged ourselves ready for the sergeant major's inspection. I shifted uncomfortably in my stiff, immaculate uniform, with its sharp creases. I looked along the line. The first thing that drew my gaze were their boots. A couple had normal boots, though I don't know when they last saw polish. A few were wearing light-green canvas jungle boots, others were in the thick boots we wore for winter, and there were even a couple of lads in desert boots.

Their crumpled shirts were similarly mismatched, coming in a range of colours I didn't even know you could find in the army. Not all of them had a tie, and those who did had secured them around their necks with eccentric knots. *Wow*, I thought, *these guys are going to get in so much trouble. This is supposed to be a parade!*

And then the sergeant major ambled in. He also looked like shit. His beret was askew, and in the corner of his mouth was a precariously balanced fag that dropped ash onto his stained uniform. He beamed at the soldiers in front of him. 'Brilliant, well done, guys. You're looking great. Right! Let's go down to the church.'

It was at that moment that they all appeared to notice me for the first time. None of them said anything, but they each gave me the amused, slightly surprised look usually reserved for someone who has turned up wearing jeans to a black-tie dinner.

A year later I found myself in Hereford again for Remembrance Day. At precisely 9.45 I clattered into the barrack block. My tatty shirt was barely tucked into a mismatched pair of trousers that had spent the last 12 months crammed into a damp cupboard. I was still doing up my tie. Four perfectly turned-out new boys stared at me in shock. 'Anybody got a poppy?'

□

The SAS becomes your life. It's all-consuming because it demands so much of you. One consequence of this is that you essentially disappear from the lives of most people you know. That's what the regiment preferred us to do. I completely lost touch with my mates in the Staffords. The idea is that as few people as possible should know who you were serving with, because it makes you and those you love less of a target. Obviously my wife knew, and there were a couple of very trusted friends that I felt comfortable telling. Otherwise I kept my own counsel. Most people, even if they suspected something, tended to respect my need to keep this important part of my existence private, or had become more wary of me, so they left me alone.

I didn't even tell my parents. Somehow, my dad knew anyway, because he always seemed to know stuff you wouldn't expect him to. I don't believe in the spirit world or anything like that, and yet I promise you this: my dad sensed things. Don't ask me to explain it, but it's true. He *knew* I'd joined the SAS long before I told him.

There were so many stories like this. Dad came to England then didn't go back to Jamaica a single time for the first 20 years he was here. I never met his parents and he rarely even talked about the island he'd left behind. And then one day he had a dream that his father was dying. So he returned home. He arrived to find his dad in good health. Getting on, but nothing more than that. He only became ill during the three weeks my dad was staying there. At some point, the cheap airline he'd flown out with went bust, which meant that the flight that was supposed to bring him back to England was cancelled. It took a week to sort out an alternative. Which was long enough for his dad to die. If he'd got the plane he was supposed to, he wouldn't have been able to say goodbye.

Strange things happened later, too. His dad would come back to him, sometimes as a ghost, sometimes in dreams. Whenever I went away to do something dangerous he'd visit and tell him, 'Your son is on a deadly mission.' There were very particular moments, or events, when my dad sensed something. He'd say, 'Oh, did something happen on such and such a date?' and I'd say, 'Yes, Dad, that's when a bomb went off while I was in Ireland.'

One time, when I was in Gibraltar, I got the chance to do some diving as part of our adventure training. I'd always hated the water, but you didn't really get much of a choice as to exactly what you did. And, anyway, I was a 17-year-old kid from a council estate; people like me didn't usually get a chance to do stuff like this. And I was being paid for it! I found out that, actually,

I loved it. Except that one morning, on a deep dive, I had a blockage in my breathing apparatus, something that I only discovered when I was already in the water. Fortunately the problem occurred before I'd gone too far down, otherwise that would have been me done for.

A few days later, I received a letter from my parents, who I hadn't spoken to for weeks, and who had no idea that I'd been diving. At the bottom was some scrawl from my dad. He'd written – or at least I'd thought he'd written – 'You've had a problem driving.' This puzzled me, I couldn't think of anything I'd experienced that matched this description. It was only when I got back and it came up in conversation that I realised it was his bad handwriting. His dad had visited him and had said that I was having trouble with my diving gear.

Like me, he wasn't a man of faith. I don't know whether he believed in any kind of formal religion, and I'm not sure how he would have categorised his experiences. But I think these visitations reassured him. And when I'd come back on leave, he'd always be desperate to see me. Because he was proud, which I know he was, but maybe also because he wanted some confirmation that his visitations had some counterpart in reality.

□

Within the first 18 months in the SAS I'd already seen and done more than in the entire 12 years of my time in the regular army. The jobs came thick and fast. It was relentless, and almost too much to process at times.

You might be away on a long jungle deployment, then the second you arrive back you're sent out to do some close protection in a suit that only just manages to hide the swollen red insect bites that cover your entire body. You're sitting there in a meeting, a pistol stuffed down your pants, staring at the other side's massive bodyguards, trying to process the fact that just a day or two earlier you were sitting in a sodden bivouac, and now you're guarding a VIP in a building so covered in gold it feels like a palace. Our enemy had been the leeches and the spiders. Here it was men whose motivations and intentions remained obscure. Every time they turned to whisper to each other, or put their hands inside the suits that, like ours, contained weapons, you'd feel a thrill of adrenaline – is it happening *now*? – that would just as quickly subside back into a hyper-focused state of alertness.

Everything was compartmentalised. Nobody goes into the SAS wanting to kill anybody. As ragged as our personal lives often were, they still existed. And we still had to go about the normal, mundane business of soldiering; kit had to be cleaned, training topped up.

But when we were called up, we had to be ready to just go. You had to be able to switch from being a normal person to being someone ready to do whatever a situation demanded. That wasn't the same as putting on your devil's horns and becoming 'the ultimate assassin'. We didn't get the red mist. It was about being able to locate that aggressive side that can eliminate a threat in a hostile environment.

Mission followed mission. I travelled the world and took part in things that I'm still really proud of. I genuinely felt as if I was at the top of my game. Then it all came crashing down.

In our troop there were two who never married (they preferred to just play around), one who stayed happily married, and the rest of us went through it. *Bang, bang, bang.* It was like dominoes.

You're away so much. Nothing is ever certain. You can't make plans. Leave is not a priority; it can get cancelled at the last minute. Your wife will know that you're going away, but not where to, or for how long. Part of your existence, a huge, significant part of it, will always be hidden from the people that are supposed to be closest to you. There's an unspoken agreement that it's all locked away in a box. I never told my missus what had happened or how it had made me feel. You don't let out any emotions.

Some people take advantage of that. They lead second lives. That was never going to be me. At the same time, even as I was thriving in my new unit, I knew that my marriage was in serious trouble.

The truth was we probably shouldn't have ever tied the knot. We only really did it because of the baby we had on the way. And then, when I joined the SAS, I was consumed by the role, because you had to be. My job always came first, and it was the thing I gave the best of myself to. I was always away, and even when I was home, my mind was elsewhere. My wife hated every minute of that existence, and I can understand why.

The time came when we realised that we were never going to be able to outrun the problems that had been with us since we'd first met. The relationship was broken, so the best thing we could do was try to emerge without being broken ourselves.

213

We agreed that we would separate, and I went to do some training in Australia.

Being in rural Australia, among the sheepshearers, miles away from everything back in England that was doing my head in and the relentless pace of squadron life, seemed to offer a welcome break.

One Saturday I went out for a quick lunchtime pint with a couple of new Aussie mates.

Drink followed drink followed drink. The chilled-out beer we'd planned turned into a proper day-long session. As evening fell, we realised we'd probably outstayed our welcome in the pub we'd been in all afternoon. 'Where can we go?' One of the blokes I was with, a skinny, slightly nervous lad, suggested a nearby hotel, so we straggled in there, suddenly feeling both unsteady on our feet and extremely hungry. None of us had eaten since breakfast. We bought beers and headed upstairs, where we found ourselves in a function room. Nobody else was in there, but there were a number of trestle tables laden with plates and plates of finger food.

We began demolishing the sandwiches and sausage rolls in front of us, our pleasure only interrupted by an angry Australian voice that had suddenly materialised just behind my shoulder. An incandescent-looking woman was standing there. 'Hey, what are you eating all that for? This is Shane's birthday.'

Oh God. Unwittingly, we'd made the first mistake of the night. The room had suddenly filled with a sea of similarly disgruntled sheepshearers. Shane's mates. They were all enormous, with forearms like Popeye's. None of them looked like they were keen for us to stay. Fair enough: nor were we.

'I'm so sorry. We didn't know.'

She started gobbing off again. 'You better not touch that.'

'OK, we're leaving, we had no idea.'

We made our way downstairs and found a bar where we could order some food.

Then, without warning, the same woman appeared, running towards us like she was on some urgent mission. 'I hope you paid for that,' she yelled, pointing at our meals. I realised that she was as drunk as we were.

'Fuck off. Of course we did.'

At this she started crying and streaked across to the biggest of the sheepshearers, who had come down to find out what the fuss was all about. She pointed at us and started gabbling into his ear, standing on tiptoes so she could reach. I saw him crack his knuckles and storm towards me. Pissed as I was, I knew danger when I saw it. I decided that he probably wasn't coming over for a polite conversation. If I didn't get in first, he was going to batter me.

I stood up and caught him in the face with a right hook. He stumbled back, holding his bleeding nose, his eyes filled with shock. He hadn't been expecting that. Still, it was only delaying the inevitable. He hurled himself at us, swinging great punches in my direction. It was like being assaulted by an angry octopus.

After a minute of two, we were pulled apart by bouncers, who suggested, in the firmest of terms, that it was probably time for us to leave. None of us were going to disagree. His mates were about to join in, so it would have got extremely ugly for us. And that should have been that. There was a taxi rank outside;

we could have been back in the barracks in minutes. But that's when we made our second mistake. 'Oh, look,' I said, there's something going on down there.' Like a lot of hotels in Australia, this one had a little casino beneath the main property, where people could gamble, watch horse-racing and drink.

'Let's get another drink,' I suggested, always the daft one. At two in the morning the casino closed and we were all booted out, just in time to crash into the sheepshearers who were just coming out of the hotel upstairs. They'd been drunk when we last saw them, now they were absolutely *steaming*. They were all giving off a feral energy, which quickly turned into rage when they saw who was standing blearily before them.

Even tidied up for a night out they still stank of grease and mutton. The muscles on their giant forearms started to pulse. *Jesus,* I thought, *nothing about this is good.* My skinny friend had obviously come to the same conclusion. One moment he was standing by my side, the next moment he'd disappeared into the night. Me and Pat, the other guy I'd been drinking with, started walking in the opposite direction. There was no way I was going to give them the satisfaction of running. After a couple of paces I stopped and turned round. They'd all followed me. *Better get this over with.*

The bloke I'd punched a couple of hours before stepped forward. Someone had made a clumsy attempt to patch his nose up but it was still crusted with dried blood. He stopped close to me, swaying menacingly, an angry giant fuelled by litres of Victoria Bitter and rum.

'Come on, mate,' he leered, 'fucking come on.'

Never back down. My dad's words came back to me, as they always did at moments like this. The bloke shoved me and my back thumped into something. I took a quick glance. It was a wire fence; there was no way out. Backing down or running away weren't really options any more.

Meaty sheepshearer's arms started raining punches down on both of us. I was trying to use everything I'd learned when I'd boxed for the Staffords and had put my hands up to try to cover myself. But blow after blow kept on falling. There was a relentlessness to their assault, like they were not going to stop until I'd been reduced to a bloody heap of broken flesh and bones. *God,* I thought, *it's going to be lights out in a minute.*

So I did the only thing that I could. I rammed my head forward then sank my teeth into the leader's chest. *Jesus,* I thought, he's muscular. There was nothing soft about this man. Still, he squealed like a pig as a bloom of red suddenly appeared on his white shirt. 'The nigger's biting me!' He pushed me away and staggered back, his face clouded by disbelief. His mates all paused too, unsure what to do next. This gave me the space I needed. I elbowed my way past them and started walking away as calmly as my hammering nerves would let me.

There was an angry stir as they collected themselves and started to move after me. *Well, at least I've bought myself some time.* Then there was the growl of an engine and a taxi pulled up. Someone flung the door open – it was Pat. 'Get the fuck in.'

I jumped into the seat, exhaling with relief. That bite, which came over two decades after the bite that had showed the school bullies that I was willing to stand up for myself, had

217

saved my life. And yet I knew, too, that not much happens in isolation.

◻

I returned to begin a spell of counter-terrorism training and a divorce process that very quickly got ugly. My wife started causing trouble for me, and our lawyers were at each other's throats. But, eventually, an agreement was reached.

This should have come as a relief, a chance to start afresh. Instead, I found myself feeling more entangled than ever. I was alone, 50 grand in debt, living in an army base, back sleeping under a rough blanket, just like I had when I was a 17-year-old recruit. Except back then I had some money in my pocket, because my dad had given me a few quid. Everything I earned was going to pay down the debt. The worst of it though, the thing that ate away at me most, was that I couldn't see my daughter.

The blokes in the regiment saw I was struggling, so they took me out on the piss. I'd tell them I was broke, but they'd tell me not to be so stupid. I'd sling back wine and beer, which I thought I needed, because I told myself I couldn't get to sleep unless I was drunk. The problem was that I'd collapse in my bed, then wake up two hours later, my brain full of my catastrophic life. I was angry, I was bitter and I was afraid. Every time I thought of the money I owed, I felt breathless with panic. Every time I thought of the daughter I wasn't able to see, I felt winded by grief.

I found myself stuck in a doom loop. Six months went by like this. For the first time since I'd been a kid I felt powerless, as if there was nothing I could do to improve my situation except to continue to drown myself with drink and hope that, one day, the misery would end.

One day, my mouth sandpaper dry, my head still woozy, I headed to the firing range. The night before had been horribly broken. I'd slept for no more than an hour or two, mostly lying there tormented by spiralling thoughts, desperately hoping for dawn.

There was usually something comforting about being on the range. For a while I could concentrate on hitting the targets in front of me and nothing else. I was able to push everything else to the back of my mind. I found myself loading a pistol, my hands performing a task that I knew so well that I no longer needed to think about it. I carried on, mechanically feeding 9mm rounds into magazines. But, gradually, the same thoughts that tore my sleep to shreds every night returned. I put a magazine in my pistol, then started putting tiny drops of gun oil into its moving parts. A minute or two went by. Almost without making a conscious decision to do so, I raised the pistol's barrel, inserting it a little way into my mouth. I felt cold metal, tasted rank, bitter oil. *What's the best way of doing this?* I asked myself. *If I fire now, it blasts my teeth out.* I moved the gun, higher, so it hovered beside my temple. *Is this a better way?*

I'd long since taken the safety catch off, now I removed the second pressure. I just needed to squeeze the trigger a fraction, no more than a hairline, and I'd send a bullet travelling at 335 metres per second into my brain. It would be over. I'd be using no more force than was required to blink.

My hands started to shake. *No,* I thought, *this cannot be how it ends.*

◻

Everything improved after that. There are times when you need a shock, something that forces you to look at your life from a different perspective. I realised that I didn't want to give up, and looking back, I'm pretty sure I'd never have gone through with it. But I also realised that I could not carry on existing as I had. What helped me is that I reminded myself of my dad's mindset: never be a victim. There are always going to be problems in life. There will always be negative people, haters. Don't let them win. Don't dwell too much on how bad a hand life has dealt you. Take responsibility for any mistakes you've made and take the consequences on the chin. You can't change the past. Instead, focus on what you can do, even if it's only something small, to make things better. For me it was fitness.

I cut booze out and started going to the gym morning, noon and night. If we got back from counter-terrorism training at midnight, I'd go to the gym. If I woke up at 4am with a racing mind, I'd go to the gym. It took my mind off what was going on, as well as giving me an outlet for all the frustration that had been building up inside me. It saved my life – it literally did.

At the same time, the regiment looked after me. I was sent on a training post on sergeant major's money, even though I was still just a corporal. (No matter what rank you have when you join the SAS, you start your life in the regiment as a trooper, then work your way back up.) That really helped, and though I didn't manage to pay off the debt immediately, I was able to chip away at it.

I wish I'd known then what I do now. It always gets better. The passage of time rubs the sharp edges off even the worst experiences. You might be going through the darkest days, but it will get better. No matter how bad your day has been, it's always going to get better. You just have to hold on for long enough. Because sometimes it's enough to just hang on in there. Don't give up, no matter how tricky or bleak things might seem. Part of the SAS's mindset is that you try to do the difficult, the impossible, because that's the last thing your enemies will expect. They think you're going to come in through the doors? OK, how do you climb up to the roof? There's always a way; you just have to put your mind to it. I'm a crap swimmer, but I reckon I could cross the Channel. It might take days, but I'd do it. Nothing's better than your attitude.

That experience means that I'll never take life for granted. Instead, I'm just desperate to thrive on everything that comes my way. It's made me more resilient and helped me understand that while you can't always win, you learn from failure in a way you never do from success. Failure's the best teacher there is.

◻

Years passed, and life carried on surprising me.

In the early afternoon of 11 September 2001, I walked into my squadron's interest room at Hereford, where a group of men were crowded around the television, and for a few seconds I struggled to believe what I was seeing. Or, more accurately, I didn't even know what I was seeing. It seemed to be a film of a huge passenger jet hurtling at great speed into what resembled a New York skyscraper, before exploding in an extravagant mushroom cloud of fire and smoke. I looked again, puzzled by the news-style tickertape running along the bottom of the screen. *So this isn't a movie?* Almost embarrassed to ask what felt like a silly question out loud, I said, to nobody in particular, 'Is this real?'

Nobody answered directly, but someone else piped up. 'Lads,' he said, 'I think we're about to get fucking busy.'

He was right, of course; 9/11 changed everything. It was a stone thrown into a pool, causing ripples that are still being felt to this day. I had no idea what sort of impact it would go on to have on my life. Or on the lives of many millions of others, a handful of whose fates would end up intertwined with mine.

But other big things happened to me that year too. Most significantly, I met Zoe, who was working behind the bar of a pub in Stoke. The first things that I noticed were that she was tall, blonde and incredibly beautiful. As I got to know her better, I realised that she was also clever, stubborn, thoughtful, affectionate, resilient and loyal. My dad, who'd sensed from the very start that something was off about my first marriage, had an instant reaction about Zoe too. 'You've got good a one here,' he told me, 'Stick with her.' He was right of course, though I'm not sure you'd need to be a psychic to spot that Zoe is the best thing that has ever happened to me. Nothing else even comes close.

We started off slowly. I remained tender after my divorce, unsure whether I'd ever be ready to marry or even have that kind of relationship again. And, of course, I was still consumed by a job that took me to strange, dangerous parts of the world for months at a time. For her part, Zoe needed to work out what sort of life she wanted to build for herself.

In the end we realised that what we had was special, even if things weren't always going to be easy. That's how I ended up leaving for Iraq in 2003 with a lock of her hair taped to the back of my escape map, and my nickname for her, 'Angel', written on the back of my helmet. Zoe stayed in Stoke, watching Sky News so obsessively that she refused to let her parents change the channel, both hoping and dreading that there would be news of the men in the special forces who had, like me, disappeared into the desert.

10

WHAT HAVE WE DONE?

Dad had been diagnosed with lung cancer in October 2002. It was the smoking that caused it. He always, always had a fag on the go. Everyone had been the same when he was young, puffing away on buses and aeroplanes and in cinemas. But while a lot of his contemporaries kicked the habit, he never stopped.

When cigarettes got more expensive, he just got people to bring back tobacco from their holidays abroad and he smoked rollies. For a long time he had a persistent cough and was persuaded to have an X-ray. I remember the doctor looking at the results and saying, 'This doesn't look good.' But Dad thought it was too late to quit.

He retired at 65, though he was never going to be someone to take things easy. If he wasn't grafting away in his garden, he'd be in the gym, the first time in his life he'd ever gone. We'd work out together when I was back on leave, watched by people who couldn't believe a man of his age could be so strong.

And then he fell sick. Shortly before he had to enter a hospice I got to spend the afternoon with him. He was lying in bed, something I don't think I ever got used to seeing, and he called me over. With a great look of pride on his face, he said, 'We've finally paid the mortgage on this place. We're leaving it, we're leaving everything to you and your brother.' I could tell how important it was to him. He arrived in this country with nothing, lived in tiny bedsits, worked his fingers to the bone in factories, pits and building sites, and now he was able to pass *something* on to his two boys.

As I left the house to make the journey down to Hereford, I remember looking back up at my parents' bedroom window. I'd sensed something, maybe a movement, I wasn't sure. The blinds were down but I could tell he'd got out of his bed. I realised I could just about make out the silhouette of his head. The proudest, best man I ever knew was watching me.

He hung on for almost another whole year, until September 2003. It was like he wanted to make sure I'd got back safely from Iraq. What was strange was that for a long time, he had been diminishing, becoming ever vaguer, like a fuzzy sketch of the person he had been. Then, right at the end, he snapped back into sharp focus.

I'd told him a while before that I was thinking about a new career, but I wasn't sure that he'd understood. Now, lying there in his hospice bed, he asked me, 'Melvyn, what are you going to do when you leave the army?' Not waiting for me to reply, he quickly rapped out a bet he wanted me to place for him, as well as giving me his lottery numbers for that weekend's draw. He looked at me impatiently, as if he couldn't understand why I hadn't already rushed out to follow his orders.

I left thinking, *He's going to live for years more.* Then, a day later, the hospice called. 'Come quick', they told me, 'he doesn't have long.' That brief swell of energy and alertness had passed. He was already a long way from us by the time I reached him.

There was a feeling that this phase might last for days, so I headed for home, but just as we were driving away I got another call. 'He's gone.'

My brother and I went back the next day and shaved him. Even to the end he had hated having stubble. As I carefully drew the razor across his cold cheek, I thought back to a conversation we'd had, not long before. 'Son,' he'd said, 'you know I'm dying.'

I wasn't thinking straight at the time. I just replied, 'Yeah, Dad, I've had loads of mates die. You'll be OK.'

At the time, I didn't understand what I'd said, why I'd let those odd words come out of my mouth. But suddenly I knew. For all my life I'd thought he would live for ever. Of course, that was wrong. He was going to die, and yet I hadn't been able to allow myself to believe that he would. Now, though, I had no choice.

Two years later, I finally left the SAS. I had never stopped loving the work, but I knew that I'd not be able to go on for ever. Zoe and I were about to start a family and I wanted to be around for my kids as much as I could. The other priority was becoming a bit more financially secure. It wasn't that long ago that I'd been divorced with £50,000 of debt hung round my shoulders. That wasn't a situation I ever wanted to go back to, or land Zoe in.

So, when a good friend, who'd left the regiment not long before, called me up to ask me if I was interested in a job providing security for CBS journalists in Baghdad, it felt like a perfect opportunity. Zoe and I came up with a plan. I'd do it for four years, working nine to ten months a year. That's how you made your money. I knew the risks involved, but as I said to Zoe, 'You know what it's been like in the SAS. You know how dangerous it's been. Once I get out, I'll keep the same mindset. You just carry on believing that I'm still in the regiment. I'll be working with regiment guys. However, this time I'll be making a shitload and we can save, save, save.'

I knew that I was stepping into a different world. If I'd died on an SAS raid the line would be, *Here's a hero who got killed fighting for his country.* If I lost my life protecting CBS journalists I knew what would be said: *He's a mercenary, he shouldn't even have been there.*

But that was the deal I was taking. Anyway, I reasoned, how dangerous could it really be?

◻

In April 2005 I arrived in a city that was boiling over with violence and rage. In the immediate aftermath of the 2003 invasion, the Americans and British had been welcomed, treated like heroes even. But in less than two years, everything had changed. The coalition had made countless mistakes. Most of all, they'd disbanded the army and sacked anybody who had been a member of Saddam's Ba'ath party. This meant that they had created a country filled with millions of impoverished former soldiers and police who'd lost their identity and self-respect while retaining their weapons and knowledge. Of course they turned against us.

Once there had been whole areas where Sunnis, Shias, Christians and Jews lived alongside each other. Under Saddam the various different groups had rubbed alongside each other. They'd intermarried, and they'd respected each other's faiths. They were safe as long as they did what the gaffer expected and kept a picture of him up on their walls. They had schools, they had structure. It was easy to walk the streets; there was little to no petty crime.

Now the country had been redrawn on sectarian lines. Each side was sending mortar bombs indiscriminately into the other side's homes. Over the next few years I'd speak to many people who told me how *glad* they'd been when we first came. They had hated Saddam. His secret police had killed members of their families. They'd been revolted by his barbarism and repression. I lost count of the people I'd talked to with horror stories. Their cousin killed; their daughter raped. Now, though, they had new ones. Guards would come in crying to work, telling us that they'd just lost family members in a car bombing, or a random assassination in the street. All of this meant they were desperate for Saddam to come back. The other stuff was forgotten, all that they remembered is that before 2003 they could go to the market without fear of a truck bomb going off, that their kids could go to school.

The job of the journalists at CBS was to try to document this rapidly deteriorating situation as fairly and accurately as possible for their viewers. My job was to try to keep them alive while they did this. Neither was easy.

Our greatest fear was always that they'd be kidnapped. This was the beginning of that time when hostages in orange jumpsuits were paraded in front of the world by Islamists posing with swords. And religious extremists weren't the only danger. Gangs of violent opportunists were always ready to try to extract a fat ransom for Westerners. And, since CBS was an American organisation, the journalists were an even more tempting target.

Iraq had become a country where everyone was in danger all of the time. Every piece of filming or reporting had to be done quickly. As soon as we arrived at the location I'd feel as if the timer was already racing, because the longer we were there, the greater the chance that a bystander would alert someone nasty who wanted to snatch an American journalist. I always wanted to be in and out in 15 minutes, so I'd try to encourage them to keep the pace of their work up. 'Come on, come on, come on, *let's go!*' As the reporter and their team worked, I'd be scanning the buildings around us for any sign of suspicious movements or individuals. As bad as the consequences of capture would be for one of our clients, I knew that our fate would be quick, unceremonious, and likely to end with our bodies being dumped in a quiet backstreet.

I learned to dread the moment when a journalist shouted, 'Cut, can we do that again?' That meant another few minutes. And sometimes you'd sense a prickle of interest in the crowd around you. It was almost like the temperature had changed. That's when you knew you really had to move, and maybe take a different route out to the one you'd driven in on.

I remember one day how we rushed to film the aftermath of a car bomb, arriving in time to see the fire brigade hose down everything that had collected in the massive crater that had just appeared in the middle of a Baghdad street. Limbs, heads and clothing were strewn over hundreds of metres. The mounds of singed or burning flesh were brushed up, there was no attempt to find DNA to identify the perpetrators, they just wanted to get the road empty again. My nose filled with the same overpowering stench I'd first smelled 15 years before, on the Basra Road. When I peered a little into the distance, I could see that windows were broken on buildings as far as the eye could see.

I suddenly noticed a red sticky pool of liquid on the pavement beside me. Looking up I saw a gory stump of a civilian, their jeans still clinging to them, lodged in a palm tree above me. As blood dripped down other locals walked past, apparently unbothered by what they'd just seen. If you ever asked people on the scene what they thought, their attitude was always, *Inshallah*. These things – signs that their society was collapsing – had become so much a part of their everyday lives that they had become fatalistic about it.

We filmed it all. By this point I had been with the team for long enough to know that this footage wouldn't make it onto the Western news. But the local channels would show it. I really respected the journalists and cameramen. Although, to be honest, I didn't know who most of the big names were. The Americans would say, their eyes gleaming with excitement, 'Diane Sawyer is coming. *Diane Sawyer*,' and I'd look blankly back at them. 'Who?'

All of them worked unbelievably hard, and they were brave too, sometimes reckless, I thought, especially when they got a sniff of a story. Then they'd be like dogs chasing a fox: completely single-minded, willing to do anything, to take any risk, to catch their prize.

Ultimately, we were working for the journalists. We could give advice, but we didn't have the authority to forbid them from doing anything. The most we could hope to do was appeal to the bureau chief and hope they'd make the journalist see sense.

As informal as things had been in the SAS, it was still part of the military, and what I came to understand quite quickly was that journalists, especially war correspondents, they're … different. It wouldn't have been appropriate for me to talk to them like I might have another bloke in the regiment. There wasn't a chain of command like before. You couldn't bellow at these journalists and order them to stay at their desks. If anything, that would make them even more determined to go.

I had come into this job as somebody who had thought of himself as being at the top of his game. And in one way, that was true. I'd risen to become a sergeant major in the SAS, an elite unit that I believed was the finest of its kind in the world. There wasn't much further I could go. But it was increasingly clear that I still had a lot to learn about how other parts of the world worked. Sometimes that's not easy to admit, especially if you've come to think of yourself as an expert in your field. Plus, I had just entered my forties, a time when most people start to get a bit more set in their ways. I could see the attraction of retreating into the safety of doing things the way I'd always done them, and thinking about the world in the way I'd always thought about the world. At the same time, though, I think that I was ready to open myself up to new perspectives, to listen to different arguments, and to tackling problems in ways that I hadn't had much use for in my old life.

It didn't matter how good my medical and navigational and military skills were, I had to find a way of getting along with the journalists. I had to work out how I could accommodate their priority (getting news stories) with my priority (keeping them alive), even when, as was often the case, those two things clashed.

I needed to be as flexible as I could be, and yet able to know when I really had to draw the line, and say, 'Sorry, there is just no way you're doing this.'

Sometimes it was enough to be firm and give them a long enough list of specific reasons. On other occasions, you just had to look for a different angle of approach. Working for Lara Logan, one of the network's stars, was a good example of this. For her, the story was more important than anything. I mean, she was *obsessed*. She also knew the power she had, and was willing to exploit it. A lot of the other guys hated working with her, because she pushed so hard. I had a good rapport with her though, and usually found a way of appealing to a side of her not everyone else could see.

She had young nieces at the time, about the same age as my daughter Amy, who'd been born in May 2005, and she was crazy about them. I remember going to talk to her on one occasion, when she was desperate to do something I thought was reckless. Before I'd even sat down she looked at me sternly. 'We're going to get this story.'

'Lara, I've just had a baby. Same age as your niece. I'd really like to see her again. I'll go out with you, 'cos that's the job. But is this one really worth it?'

She smiled at me. 'OK, Mel, you're right on this one.'

But I couldn't always persuade her to listen to me. One of my most frightening experiences was our journey with Lara to meet a senior figure in the insurgency at an undisclosed location somewhere in Sadr City.

Sadr City was one of the most dangerous areas of one of the most dangerous cities in the world. Large parts of it were controlled by Shia cleric Muqtada al-Sadr's Mahdi Army, a powerful and ruthless militia that had emerged since the invasion had plunged the country into chaos.

It was a place where gunmen routinely shot and killed their opponents on the street, or detonated car bombs outside crowded restaurants. The discovery of 13 murdered Iraqis in a shallow grave that year was unusual only because of the scale of the brutality. They'd all been bound, gagged and shot multiple times.

When the Americans went into the area, they had to do so in force. The risk of taking casualties, or, worse, having one of their troops kidnapped would otherwise have been too great. Generally, though, the coalition left the people of Sadr City to their own devices. What else could they do, blow up the place?

One of our fixers had come to Lara with the proposal. There were assurances that we'd be kept safe, but a lot of journalists had been told similar things and ended up in a stinking prison cell. Still, Lara was dead keen. I think she knew what an amazing opportunity this was for a journalist like her. I'd done as much as I could to dissuade her, and yet she was adamant: 'We can trust them.' Nobody else seemed willing to back me up, so here we were. Our instructions were short and simple. We were given a location to drive to. When we reached it, a vehicle would make itself known, and we were to follow it.

We set off in two cars through the choking traffic in the centre of Baghdad, then wound our way through the dense maze of streets that led north-east to Sadr City. Even on supposedly safer journeys, I'd always been wary of driving through the city like this. Sometimes we went along roads that were so narrow that I knew we wouldn't be able to turn around if something went wrong.

I hated that because when you were static, stuck in traffic, or just halted by one of the thousand and one things that could block roads during that time, you were a target. Suddenly you'd notice people looking a bit differently at you. Some would peer into the car. If you saw shock on their face, you were probably going to be OK. It was when they looked and looked and looked, as if making sure of something, then strode purposefully off in another direction that you knew you might be in trouble.

The car carried on. It was a Mercedes saloon, something that we hoped would help us pass through Baghdad unnoticed. We had made a conscious decision to avoid the high-profile 4x4s favoured by contractors like Blackwater. They drove around in big groups of armoured vehicles with guns on top. That's what it took to keep embassy staff or NGO workers safe. But they also made you stand out, which wasn't what the press wanted.

Our cars were older, smaller and looked more battered. They had a certain amount of armour plating and tinted windows, but then so did vehicles owned by a lot of the richer Iraqis. Nobody who just glanced at us would notice anything unusual.

The streets were busy. Crowds either side of the road pressed against us. I checked my mirror; the vehicle carrying Lara was still behind. We tried to avoid looking like a convoy, because that drew attention. But you always wanted to keep the other car close, so you could stay in touch with each other. I looked out of the window at the city's shabby tower blocks. Most were a dull khaki, though occasionally I'd catch sight of one of the murals depicting Muqtada al-Sadr or another cleric staring menacingly at us, against a background of blazing colour. These vied for space with equally garish adverts written in Arabic. It was often hard to work out what they were actually selling, or who, here, could afford to buy their products. Kids played football, black-clad women hurried back from the market laden with shopping, men in old shirts and baggy trousers smoked mournfully. Somehow, the normality of the scene heightened my sense of anxiety about what we were doing.

At some point I realised that I couldn't remember the last time I'd seen an American soldier or checkpoint. We had passed over the border into Sadr City. From this point, each metre we travelled was a metre further from anybody who could help us if events took an unpleasant turn.

Our vehicle carried on making its way deeper and deeper into the suburb until we arrived at our destination. Before we'd even come to a halt, a large black BMW pulled out in front of us. He didn't need to identify himself; this was clearly our man.

'That's him,' I said, pointing it out to the driver. 'Keep close to him.' He was a good guy; he spoke almost no English and was silent, but he knew the city. The BMW started weaving through a series of increasingly narrow streets. Up until now, I'd been trying to track our progress on one of the basic maps we used to coordinate our runs to and from the airport, but I quickly gave up. The route we were being taken was bewildering, probably by design. I had no idea where we were.

I looked up. We were now surrounded by a fleet of almost identical black BMWs whose presence ensured we wouldn't be able to turn back. The time to have second thoughts had long since passed.

As always, we'd brought our weapons with us. When we were out and about we transported the American M4 rifles we'd had to procure for ourselves because our employers had been too mean to buy us proper weapons in tripod bags so that we'd just look like normal members of the film crew. Now, though, the rifle nestled snuggled in the footwell of the car. If things got nasty, I'd be able to grab it in a split-second. My pistol was in a holster tucked into my trousers. I stretched my hands to reassure myself that I'd be able to reach it.

For the first time that day I thought, *They're going to break their promise.* A few minutes passed. I'd been cycling through our options, trying to see if there was any way we could escape if we discovered we'd been lured into a trap. But there was nothing; we were at their mercy. The car in front slowed down and stopped in the street. Our driver looked at me, as if asking, *Should I do the same?* I nodded at him. I could see he was as afraid as we were, and yet it wasn't as if we had much of a choice.

Armed men appeared beside our door, indicating that we were to get out of our car. As soon as we'd all clambered out, we were searched and they removed our weapons and radio equipment. Next they painstakingly inspected our vehicles, to establish if we'd hidden any bombs inside them. Again I looked around, at the washing hung from people's windows, at a little stall selling oranges, and felt a peculiar sense of surprise that for others, life was hurrying on as usual.

The men searching us were polite and efficient, but I could see how much they hated me each time one of them looked in my direction. I wondered what reserves of self-control they were having to draw on to keep themselves from putting a couple of bullets in the back of my skull.

It reminded me of a funeral we'd gone to film recently. They were burying six people who'd been hit by an American helicopter the day before while trying to plant IEDs. They stared at us with burning eyes, the anger and resentment so thick in the hot Middle Eastern air that I almost choked on it. Weeping men were gripping their weapons tightly, clearly desperate to take revenge. That day, our survival had felt as if it rested on a hairline chance. It wouldn't have taken much to change that hatred into violence.

It felt similar now. Standing there, conscious that I no longer had any way of protecting myself or the people I was employed to keep safe, I suddenly felt incredibly vulnerable. One of the men, obviously the most senior, fired a volley of questions at our translator who replied in an anxious, wavering voice. 'What did he want to know?' I asked after the insurgent had turned to talk to a couple of his men, obviously satisfied by our translator's response. 'He was trying to establish if we'd been followed. I put his mind at rest.'

There was more talk, then we were all blindfolded and bundled into a new set of cars that had pulled up as we were being searched. For an hour we drove in complete silence, the only sign that we were still in the city the muffled sounds of street life that occasionally burst in on us. Fear mounted inside me with every second that passed. Control over this situation had long since been snatched out of our hands. I realised that I had not been so completely at the mercy of other human beings since the final stages of selection, when we had been subjected to a simulated interrogation. The difference then, of course, was that the people holding me captive were just playing roles. The silence maintained by the driver and those guarding us began to feel ever more sinister. My mind began to fill with gruesome scenarios. I pictured all the different ways in which they might kill me. *Poor Zoe – I'd be leaving her alone with a baby and a fat mortgage, and for what, a news story?* Finally, we stopped and our blindfolds were removed.

I blinked, trying to accustom my eyes to the bright sun that seemed to be shining on us with a greater force than I had ever known. We'd arrived in a beautiful compound surrounded by walls so high that it was impossible to see over them. It was like being in an embassy, or the Green Zone.

Usually, when we went to places like this, we'd be given food, or a cup of tea. Usually, Arabs pride themselves on their hospitality. But while Lara was ushered inside, where she stayed for two hours, we were left to stew, watched by men who visibly seemed to be fantasising about how they were going to disembowel us. I don't think a minute went by when I didn't think, *They are going to take us away and murder us.* Occasionally I'd shoot a glance at my mate, and he'd grimace at me as if to say, *What can we do?*

And then, without warning, Lara emerged, ecstatic at having secured a great story. We were blindfolded again, before being driven on the same mazy route back to where our cars had been left. As I watched our escorts' black vehicles disappear into the mass of traffic behind us, I felt a great wash of relief. *How the hell*, I asked myself, *did we come out of that alive?*

□

What made things even more dangerous was how frightened and trigger-happy the Americans were.

I could empathise with these poor young soldiers who just wanted to get home in one piece. They were losing people left, right and centre. Suicide bombers were driving up to their checkpoints and detonating themselves. If I'd been in their position, I'd have been terrified of every vehicle. But some of the big private security firms were getting away with literal murder, and almost nothing was said about this.

Both them and the American military would drive around in vehicles plastered with signs in English and Arabic that read, 'Keep 100 metres away or we shoot.'

The idea was that if somebody did approach them, there would be time to first put on their lights and sirens, then set off flares and fire a warning shot over their heads, depending on whether they stopped or not. Only after all these steps had been taken could they engage. The problem was that when they hurtled around Baghdad in their big convoys, lights flashing, sirens blaring, there wasn't time for every civilian to get out of their way. What about the little old lady turning onto a junction just as they pass by, so that she ends up just metres away. Very often, the kid, fresh out of the States, sitting there with a big gun in his hands, frozen by fear, panicked. To him there was a clear and present danger and no time to go through the formalities. He would just let rip. That's how scared they were of car bombs. And they knew they could get away with it, because there wouldn't be an investigation.

I had my own taste of this a couple of times. Once, it was us at the junction that landed us too close to a convoy of Humvees. As soon as they spotted us, they started firing. If we hadn't been in a car with armoured glass, we'd have been killed on the spot. A few seconds later they were gone. It made me wonder how many times they had done this and the people in the car *hadn't* walked away.

On another occasion, we had two cars going through the checkpoint that led into an American camp. My friend was in the front vehicle, I was in the rear one. It was a checkpoint we'd been through before that day to drop our clients off, so they should have recognised us, but there was a new boy in charge.

To help identify us, we always travelled with an A4-sized British flag in the door that we pressed against the windscreen as we approached before we showed them the US Department of Defense passes that hung from our necks. It was just something easy to reassure them if they got spooked by seeing an Iraqi driver in the front seat.

We pulled up to the checkpoint, and without any warning an American sitting on top of a Humvee manning a machine-gun fired a .50 calibre bullet through the window of our first car. Convinced my friend and his driver had been killed, and worried that I was next, I leaped out of my vehicle, my hands high above my head. With relief I saw my mate do the same.

The gunfire brought a handful of Americans running out from the base. I looked up at the kid on the Humvee. He was a skinny lad, who looked no more than 15 years old. His face was white with fright.

I caught his eye. 'Did you not see the flag on our windscreen?'

He shook his head, 'I don't know what country that is.'

After that, we replaced our Union Jack with the Stars and Stripes.

Slowly but surely, these experiences were changing me and the way I looked at the world. We had never had to deal with anything like this in the military. We didn't need to see those ordinary tragedies. It gave me a different perspective. I lost the tunnel vision I'd once had and began to see things more clearly. Day after day, I was being shown the terrible consequences of an invasion I'd participated in. The more time I spent in Baghdad, the more I began to say to myself, *God almighty, what have we done?*

11

THE MOST DANGEROUS
PLACE IN THE WORLD

This shift in my perspective was accelerated by the fact that I was living and working beside local people. CBS had the whole third floor of the Hotel Al-Mansour, a kilometre north of the Green Zone on the banks of the Tigris. At intervals, mortar shells arced above our heads, headed for the international enclave. Occasionally they fell short, landing somewhere in the hotel's grounds, a reminder that in Baghdad death could come from anywhere at any time.

The hotel had been built in the seventies and barely been touched since. Though it did have a ghoulish recent history. The staff told me that Uday Hussein, Saddam's psychotic son, used to come here on the hunt for women to rape. High on an extravagant cocktail of drugs, alcohol and power, he'd often end the night by chucking people off the top of the building, 12 storeys up.

Now, its carpets were worn, the paint was tired, the windows were lined with tape to stop sand creeping in, and the air conditioning was so ineffective that the only way to get cool was to lie on your bed, as still as you could, while blasting yourself with a fan. Sometimes the power would go off suddenly, and we'd have rely on our emergency generators.

A lot of its 300-odd rooms were empty. But there were decent facilities; they had tennis courts at the back, as well as a

swimming pool and a gym. We shared the building with a handful of other news crews, plus some embassy staff.

At the heart of the CBS operation was its bureau chief, the
legendary Larry Doyle. This big bear of a man, who had served
in the American Marines in Vietnam before he'd become a journalist, quickly became like a father to me at a time when I was
still grieving the death of my dad. He gave me so much, and did
so much for me, just as he did for anyone who worked for him.
In return, I handed him a passion for Stoke City football club. I
don't know if that was a fair swap. Whenever I think of him, it's
always those moments when he'd ask, his voice deep, his humour
sandpaper dry, 'Oh, what's this? How *is* the soccer going?'

What I loved about him was that he looked after everyone
the same. From the kid making the tea to the guy who managed
his fleet of vehicles. Years later, he saved so many lives by securing visas for the Iraqis who'd worked for him, and their families,
to move to the States. He wouldn't leave any man behind.

Somehow, amid the chaos of the city, he always managed
to radiate calm. No crisis, no highly strung journalist, no explosion, ever seemed to rattle him. Maybe it was the cigarettes he
smoked constantly, or the two beers he'd allow himself each
night, or perhaps it was just the fact that over the course of his
40-year career he'd seen and done everything.

The other essential element in helping CBS operate in Baghdad, beyond the journalists and camera crews, was the host of
locals who lived and worked alongside us in the hotel. They
were interpreters, fixers and seekers of information, people who
understood the country in a way none of us ever could. A lot

of them had once been lawyers or doctors. One had even flown MiGs in the Iraqi air force, and had the Breitling watch that Saddam Hussein had personally handed him to prove it. They spoke good English and, having been forced to watch their economy collapse, needed to make a living any way they could. Like me, when they started working for Larry they probably knew nothing about the business of making news, but nothing could have happened without them.

The two local managers were a pair of chain-smoking brothers, former officers from the Republican Guard, who Larry had met after the First Gulf War, and kept in touch with ever since. Raz, in particular, was a great lad, even if you did sometimes wonder whether he might actually be crazy. One time, somebody was firing at our hotel. He went straight to the rooftop, picked up his automatic rifle and started spraying bullets in the general direction of our assailants while shouting 'Fuckers! Fuckers!' at the top of his voice. This done, he returned to our floor, picked up his cigarette and continued the conversation the firing had interrupted.

It was probably for the best that his calmer brother, Faz, was ultimately in charge. They arranged all of our local security, our drivers and their vehicles. The two brothers were a similar age to me and I liked talking to them. They told me what it had been like under Saddam and we swapped war stories. It was always tempting to wonder if, 15 years before, fate had thrown us onto the same battlefield. We never quite worked this out.

I loved being able to spend time with all the interpreters and guards. There were two lovely boys called Saif. One was the tea boy, which meant he was constantly running around. That was a tough gig. Whenever he came up to me to ask if I wanted tea, I'd say, 'Yeah, but I'll make it.' That way, he could sit down, and I got to have a chat.

The other Saif was the son of one of the main door guards, who'd got a job as a guard inside the hotel. What he really wanted, though, was to be a rapper like his idols on MTV. Every time he'd see me his face would light up. 'Mel! 50 Cent! Jay-Z!' Then he'd break out a few rhymes and I'd join in with him.

Anwar Abbas Lafta was one of the interpreters I was closest to, though everyone there felt affectionate towards him. That's just the sort of person he was. He was in his thirties, though looked older, with dark hair that was already thinning on top and a little potbelly that stood out from his otherwise skinny frame. Like almost everyone in Iraq, he smoked constantly, lighting one fag from the butt of the next, which left his teeth a deep shade of nicotine yellow. And like most people out there, he couldn't understand my attachment to Stoke City. 'Stoke City? No good. No good. Why don't you support a good team, like Manchester United?'

Occasionally he'd be able to go back to his own home in the city to see his family. Like me, he had young kids. We'd swap baby stories and talk about the occupation. He had a generous mind and respected what the Americans had tried to do, even as he despaired of their many mistakes and misunderstandings of his country's culture. I think the friendship we had was strengthened by the fact we both had taken jobs that took us away from the people we cared about most.

I'd often eat with my Iraqi comrades. The best times were when once a month they made a special plate of chicken and rice for all of us to share, and we'd all dig in with our hands. We'd talk about football and our families; if we were in the mood we might even have a bit of a dance together. When one of them had had a kid, I'd bring them a little present from home.

The bonds I formed with these guys was another factor in the ways in which I was changing during this time. I could feel my empathy growing, because I was being exposed to different perspectives. I'd been to so many countries during my time in the SAS, and yet I barely knew them, or the people who inhabited them, because our operations were so narrowly focused. We weren't encouraged to think that much about civilians; as long as they were safe, we weren't too interested in them. Now I was talking to these guys day in, day out, I stopped seeing them as caricatures. I enjoyed learning about the things that were different about us, even as we were able to make connections through all of the stuff that we already shared.

By contrast, a number of my colleagues were a bit stand-offish; for some reason they never felt able to trust the locals. That was their loss. I see the same attitude in a lot of ex-military guys. They don't like Muslims. They don't like Iraqis. I think a lot of that was simply because they'd never actually been embedded with them properly, or lived side by side. Safe as it was, the Green Zone was also an unreal bubble.

◻

The months went by. I realised that you can get used to anything after a while. It doesn't take long for even outlandish, unpleasant situations to start to feel entirely normal.

I wasn't as fatalistic as the Iraqis, and yet I no longer registered things like truck bombs exploding nearby, or stray bullets hitting our hotel, as unusual events. They were as much part of life in this city as the bazaars and relentless heat. I remember being on the phone to Zoe around this time. 'What's that noise?' she asked, sounding concerned. For a second I tried to work out what she was talking about, then I realised: a gun battle had erupted a few streets away – I'd simply stopped noticing.

Beyond that, I was in a good rhythm with a job that I was beginning to believe was important and useful in ways that went beyond me just earning money. Most of all, I was surrounded by a group of people who I loved spending time with, and who were having a deep impact on how I saw the world.

I think that's why some of the things that happened over the next couple of years hit me so hard.

One of the cameramen I got on best with was a brilliant guy called Paul Douglas, a committed Arsenal fan who worked closely with a soundman called James Brolan, another great bloke. Paul was small and mixed-race like me, but about a thousand decibels louder. You always knew when he was around, because you could hear him from 30 kilometres away. When we weren't working, we liked to have a bit of fun with each other. That was the sort of atmosphere Larry helped create.

I had a favourite mug. It was a clever thing that kept your brew warm for ages. Something that was arguably a bit more useful in the middle of a freezing desert than in the sweltering heat of Baghdad, but I loved it. Then one day it mysteriously disappeared. I started asking around, 'Anybody seen my mug?'

Nobody seemed to know anything. Then somebody started pushing ransom notes under my door. This was getting a bit much. 'Where's my fucking mug, boys?'

That was when they showed me the video. Paul called me into the engineer's room, looking worried. A lot of the journalists were there, their faces doomy. 'Something's come in. I think you should see it.' *Oh God, this feels serious.* The tape started rolling. A man with his face wrapped in a white hotel sheet sat in the middle of the screen, surrounded by other masked men, speaking in suspiciously familiar Arabic and pretending they had weapons. 'Is that *you*, Saif?' My rapper mate did an unconvincing impression of someone who had absolutely no idea what I was asking him about.

In the middle was my mug, wrapped in orange tape to make it look as if it was in a prisoner's jump-suit. The guy in the white sheet put on a menacing voice: 'Give us money or the mug gets it.'

I looked up at Paul. 'You bastard.'

The thing about Paul was he was on the CBS staff in London, he wasn't like the freelancers who were here because the money was good. So he didn't need to be in Baghdad, and wasn't paid much extra when he did come. Like me he loved the people and knew that the journalists were producing stories that needed to be broadcast. He and I would always try to make sure that we were out in the city at the same time.

In late May 2006 I had a spell of leave at home. I remember popping my head round Paul's door to tell him I was off. 'It's just a short stint, I'll be coming back next week.' He beamed at me. 'Mel, come and give me a big hug.' We embraced, then I rushed off to catch my plane.

Two days later, my phone rang when I was at the till in some mad jewellery shop in the Potteries in Stoke, buying a present for Zoe. I picked up, it was my friend. 'Have you heard?'

'No.' Instantly I felt a stab of alarm.

'There was a car bomb. It blew Paul and James to pieces. They died instantly. I'm really sorry, mate.'

All I could say was, 'Fuck.' The woman serving me looked shocked. I waved at her mutely and struggled to the nearest chair where I sat for what seemed like ages, trying to process the news. The grief winded me, and only seemed to mount as I learned more about their fates.

The worst of it was that they hadn't needed to go out on that job; they could have got away with just broadcasting from the roof. It was Memorial Day, and they were embedded with an American unit; the idea was that they would get footage of what the soldiers were up to over the holiday. But they got diverted en route to the base to inspect a checkpoint. What they didn't know was that the unit had been to the same checkpoint three times already, at exactly the same time each day. The insurgents had a bomb waiting. Kimberley Dozier, the journalist they were with, was also injured badly in the explosion. That she survived is a miracle. Speaking about the incident, CBS president Sean McManus called Iraq 'the most dangerous place in the world'. It was hard to disagree.

◻

But life carried on, because it had to. We still had a job to do. People came and went. In 2006 a South African cameraman, a hippyish white guy with dreadlocks called Ryan, stayed with us for a six-week stint. We got into a nice arrangement where we trained in the gym with each other. Even though we were on the hotel grounds, he was still a client that needed to be protected, so I'd take a bumbag with my pistol and radio with me, just in case. One evening we arranged to meet at eight the following morning to do a workout before were due to go out on a job at 10.30.

I went to bed sober (we didn't drink while we were in Baghdad, for obvious reasons) at a sensible time, and emerged at eight, ready to go. My mate who was on shift greeted me. 'Where are you off to?'

'I'm going to the gym with Ryan.'

'Good luck with that, they've been up all night. He's not going anywhere this early.'

The poor bloke was in a wretched state: eyes red, breath smelling like a distillery. After I'd woken him up he begged for an extra half hour to recover. I checked my watch: *Yeah, we can still make it.* 'I'll see you at eight thirty.' Although I was a bit pissed off that Ryan was still wallowing in bed, the extra time gave me the opportunity to download some photos of my daughter Amy that Zoe had sent me, a process that I'd started about two hours earlier on the hotel's painfully slow internet.

At half eight I went to Ryan's room again, but he still wasn't ready. Can we leave it till at least nine o'clock?

'God, come on, mate, we haven't got much time.'

He looked at me beseechingly. I remembered how much a hangover can sting.

'OK, fine.' Maybe I would see a lovely baby picture before we went out into the city that day!

Five minutes later, I was sitting at the little desk in my room, looking out of the patio doors that led onto a balcony, which in turn faced a big wall. It wasn't much of a view. I ate a banana, then something came over me. I decided I couldn't wait any longer. I called Ryan's room. 'I'm going down *now*.' He'd obviously had a bit of a recovery, because he agreed to come immediately.

Down we went. I'd just got my leg through the door of the gym, a small building separate from the rest of the hotel, when an enormous explosion shook everything. I stood there in shock for a couple of seconds. Ryan, who was already inside, made as if to leave the gym, so I pulled him back: 'Watch it, there could be more coming, just wait.' Then I got onto the radio. 'It's Mel, I'm OK. Client's OK in the gym. Are you OK? I'm coming up now.' I looked at my watch. It was exactly quarter to nine.

We walked back to the third floor, still puzzling over the explosion. In the absence of any obvious or immediate threats, I decided to step into my room. Maybe the photos would finally be ready. *What on earth?* Shattered glass was everywhere, glinting evilly in the morning sun. *What has happened here?* I picked my way through the shards and poked my head through the ragged shreds of what just a few minutes earlier had been my patio door.

I was still struggling to understand what had happened. Then I looked more closely at the wall opposite. Something had taken a big chunk out of the concrete. Suddenly I had it. A piece of shrapnel must have slammed into the wall, then ricocheted into my room. But where had it gone? I turned back inside. And there it was. The chair I'd been sitting in as I downloaded the photograph had an ugly tear through its back. I shivered at the idea that if I'd been there just minutes earlier, it would have scythed through my flesh. My gaze followed the trajectory I'd guessed the shards of metal would take. Sitting on the floor beneath the table was a jagged grey piece of military shrapnel, four inches by four inches in a V shape. This wasn't a weapon improvised from nuts and bolts.

Instinctively I bent to pick it up. *Bollocks*, I snatched my hand away as the room filled with a faint tang of singed flesh. The thing was still white hot.

Later, when the metal had cooled down and we'd discovered its source – a Katyusha rocket that had landed in the hotel grounds – I showed the bureau chief, a woman who'd temporarily replaced Larry, explaining about the weird, insistent desire to leave I'd had. She did a double-take. 'Fucking hell, Mel, somebody's looking after you there.'

□

By June 2007 we'd been at the Mansour for over two years. And all the time, as it had for so much of the last two decades of my career, ordinary life carried on without me. That year my son, Sam, named after my dad, had joined Amy, born in one of the coldest winters anyone in Britain could remember. I struggled being so far away from them; my contact with home was limited to phone calls.

I could tell myself that everything I was doing I was doing for them, but that didn't always make it easier. Sometimes I'd call, wanting to talk about the car bomb that had just exploded, or a near miss we'd just had, and I'd hear an edge in Zoe's voice. In the background, Sam would be chucking food across the room, Amy would be stubbornly refusing to get ready for her bath, and I would remember that Zoe was alone, dealing with our finances, the house, all the stuff that was the foundation of the life we were building together. Those were always the most important things. Whatever I was feeling suddenly faded into the background.

Coming back after a spell at home was hard. There would always be a moment as my departure approached when Zoe would catch me looking at her and our kids and just going quiet. She'd say, 'I can tell what you're thinking.' I didn't need to say it out loud. I was a stew of emotions, really. There was a big part of me that was looking forward to getting out there, catching up with the people I had come to care about so much. Another part, though, was revolted by the idea. I feared hearing news of more deaths. I hated the idea of seeing another guard in tears because they'd just learned that a cousin had been shot. This feeling that I shouldn't be there was intensified by the really distinct smell Baghdad had: a compound of sweat, heat and decay. For the first couple of days after each return, I'd be sickened by it. *God almighty,* I'd think. *I'm back here.* Then I'd just switch on. There would be a journalist to meet at the airport and escort back to the hotel, and an urgent news story would see us sprinting to our cars, ready to cross the city. By the middle of the first week, I was completely back in the game.

At the Mansour we'd almost made our peace with the fact that although we'd managed to make our own floor as safe as we could, there was little we could do to tighten up security in the rest of the hotel. The main gate remained as porous as it ever had, and despite our best efforts, they'd refused to install a metal detector at the entrance. Instead, they had a wand that from time to time they'd wave in the general direction of visitors.

Their attitude seemed to be that the fact that something hadn't happened yet was an endorsement of their methods. I called it dumb luck. Still, in one sense they were right, the worst that had happened since we'd moved in were a few misdirected mortar rounds landing in the grounds.

◻

We'd just got back to the hotel having dropped off a correspondent with the military unit they were embedded with and were about to head upstairs. As we entered I nodded to Saif the aspiring rapper, who was on duty that day, and he grinned back. We crossed the lobby and I noticed that next to a bloke and his young daughter in their bathing suits was a group of smartly dressed Iraqis conducting a meeting. They had the air of men who were connected to the government. This had been happening more and more recently, and I didn't like it; it made us more of a target.

Still, what could I do? Once we'd got back onto our floor I made myself busy in my room, sorting out some admin work I'd allowed to pile up. But 20 minutes later, there was a massive explosion somewhere below us. The whole building shook. *This doesn't sound good.*

When I hurried downstairs I was greeted by a scene of total carnage. It was as bad as anything I'd seen since we'd arrived.

Blood and body parts mixed promiscuously with shards of shrapnel. There was broken glass everywhere. Every window and door had been shattered and severed wires hung drunkenly from a ceiling that had been ravaged by the blast. The little girl had been vaporised, the only signs that she'd ever existed a few scraps of her hand that lay beside fragments from her bikini and a tattered toy dog. Those that had survived screamed in agony and shock.

There was no sign of the single suicide bomber who had walked in past any number of guards and detonated a vest under his shirt containing a small amount of plastic explosives and a cocktail of nails, nuts and bolts.

But poor young Saif had been horribly wounded. Larry wanted him taken to a Green Zone hospital; he knew Saif would die if he was abandoned in one of the local ones. To begin with, the Americans in charge refused, saying that he wasn't one of 'theirs'. That's when Larry started shouting. Not long after, Saif got a bed in an American hospital, where he was patched up before going on to Jordan for treatment and then the States for rehabilitation.

That was the end for us at the Mansour too. It had become too dangerous. Not long after that, we moved to a compound a few kilometres away, where we could look after all of our own security arrangements.

I'll never forget the sheer horror of that hotel lobby. And yet I'll also always remember Larry's insistence on securing the best possible care for Saif. Integrity – another one of David Stirling's values – is one of those qualities that is sometimes difficult to describe, and yet you know it when you see it.

Almost everything Larry did was imbued with integrity. He had a sense of what was right and wrong, and that ethos guided both his actions and his words. It would have been easier for him to have handed Saif over to one of the local hospitals, and yet he fought and fought until he'd got him the best care he possibly could. Anyone who knows him will have similar stories.

In many ways, my dad was the same. His view was that if somebody was in need, you crossed over the road to help them. I don't know if behaving like that will ever guarantee that you'll get the job you want. It doesn't pay for a big house, or lavish holidays. But it does buy you something else: the knowledge that you've made a difference to other people's lives. And I think that every time you do that, in some small way your own becomes richer, more worth living.

□

We were all still trying to get to grips with the implications of the suicide bomber's attack and Saif's injuries when we were hit by another tragedy.

Because Raz and Faz had a bit more money and influence than the blokes they employed, they'd been able to get their families out of Baghdad and to the safety of Jordan. But that wasn't an option for the majority of the Iraqis we worked alongside. Every so often they'd slip away to see their families, but that was always a risk: the fact that they worked for us made them targets for kidnapping, or murder. They were in just as much danger from the gangs who wanted to make ransom money as they were from militias who hated anybody who worked with Westerners. I think we all believed that the day would come soon when we lost one of them. People were dying and disappearing every day. It was a matter of when, not if.

Then, in August 2007, I heard the news that we'd all been fearing for a long time. 'Anwar's been kidnapped.' There was a ransom note. The policy was that we didn't pay, but even if we had been willing, it probably wouldn't have made any difference. I remember Raz shaking his head, sadly. 'They will already have killed him, there's no point.'

He was right. We'd later learn that a death squad of eight heavily armed men had gone to Anwar's house. Anwar was always a spirited human being, and this didn't change even in his last moments. He knew what these men coming to his door meant, and tried to fight back, even though he must have known he stood little chance. He was still resisting as they forced him into an unmarked white Land Cruiser. Anwar's brother had grabbed a weapon and tried to rescue him, but in the firefight that followed, their sister was shot in the arm. After that the kidnappers sped off.

They tortured Anwar before murdering him and chucking him on a rubbish dump. It was senseless. It hurt to think how vulnerable he and all the other interpreters, drivers and translators were, and yet I knew we could not protect them. What was happening in this city was too big, too cruel, too chaotic for any of us to control. The heartbreak of this, and all the other tragedies that preceded it, sometimes felt too much to bear. I'd seen my share of death in the armed forces, especially once I'd made it into the SAS. Every time a bloke died I'd be affected, because they were my comrades. But that was part of the job. We'd all signed up to fight in a unit that went on the most dangerous operations; we were trained to deal with those situations; we were armed heavily. People like Anwar had none of these advantages. Desperation had driven him, and others like him, to work for us. He had to find a way of feeding his family. The tragedy was that it was precisely this that put him and the people he cared about most in danger. That knowledge was difficult for me to bear.

12

THEY'LL REALLY SORT YOU OUT

As my time in Iraq drew on, I started to notice that the sorts of people travelling out there to do security work was changing.

There was a lot of money swishing around, at least there was if you were running one of the big companies. This did weird things to people. I knew of at least a few ex-regiment guys who'd gone into business together as mates, and before long were at each other's throats. In at least one instance I knew about, the three founder members of an outfit were all too afraid to leave Baghdad in case one of their partners swooped in and snatched their share of the business.

The bigger problem was that the riches on offer tempted a lot of people who should have known better into compromising their standards. Men who had once boasted of their integrity were now willing to send any old idiot to Iraq if it meant they could secure a fat contract.

I could see it happening across the board. That desire to get bums on seats meant standards were being watered down. Suddenly it didn't matter that the new recruits didn't have special forces experience, or had never been in combat, because nobody was checking CVs. You had people who had briefly been corporals leading whole teams, you had people whose experience was limited to being a chef way behind the lines being handed assault rifles and combat vests.

Who cared about the truth? What mattered to the men and women sitting in London, or New York, wasn't the safety or quality of the people they sent to work for them, it was the bottom line. That's why they gave gigs to so many Filipinos and Eastern Europeans: they were paying them pennies. The thing is, though, if you don't pay for quality, you don't get quality results. You just get terrified men who are out of their depth shooting everything up and getting clients killed. Look what happened with Blackwater. In 2007 some of their contractors who were supposed to be escorting a US embassy convoy started firing on civilians, killing 17 and injuring 20 more, in circumstances which are still contested to this day.

The other issue this created was that it fundamentally shifted the balance of power between the client and the men charged with guarding them. The clients were the gold mine. Contractors who complained didn't last long – their employers knew that they could always find somebody to fill the vacancy. While news organisations usually insisted on being guarded by people with special forces background, few of the other civilian outfits were as picky. For them, one man with a gun was as good as any other. Contractors across the country were being pushed into doing things they knew carried an unacceptable level of risk. But they were also afraid of doing their jobs, so most of the time they agreed. This led to horrible situations.

This is all quite a long way of beginning to explain why, towards the end of my time in Iraq, I ended up stranded in a

4x4 that was trapped in soft sand, watching helplessly as a horde of angry insurgents drew closer and closer to where I stood, and thinking: *I am done.*

◻

It all began because CBS was replacing one security firm with another, which left me temporarily unemployed. I filled the gap by taking another, short-term contract.

The job was taking a pair of American engineers to the Anbar region, a large tract of territory in the country's west. Ideally we'd have gone by helicopter, the surest way of avoiding the attention of the assorted bandits, kidnappers and religious fanatics that had rendered that area – and many like it – so dangerous.

But instead, I was assured, I'd be getting the next best thing.

I remember the conversations that led to me agreeing to the job.

'Who will I have with me?'

'Don't worry, man. You'll be the team leader. You'll have another couple of expats with you. And then a number of Iraqis. All really professional guys, you'll have the best, believe me.'

'How well-trained are the Iraqis?'

'They're really switched on. Everybody knows the drill.'

'What about kit?'

'Yeah, no worries there, mate; they'll really sort you out.'

They'd promised the world. Maybe I was naïve to trust somebody else's word, but that's what I was used to. If someone in the regiment made a promise, they kept it. Because who didn't value their integrity?

◻

CHAPTER 12

A few days later, when I turned up in the Green Zone to meet my team, I discovered that I'd been sold a pup.

The first guy I was introduced to was our medic, a garrulous Canadian called Dylan.

Dylan, who was only in his early thirties, was a good talker, I'll give him that. Once he got started, there was little you could do to arrest the flow of boasts and claims. If he'd done even a quarter of the things he said he had he'd have been one of the greatest healers on the face of the earth. But you just needed to scratch the surface to realise that it was all smoke and mirrors. He'd never been to war, and a few questions revealed that he knew next to nothing about his trade. He was just an empty vessel whose experience was limited to a spell as a part-time medic in the Canadian Army. When I asked to look at his kit I was horrified to discover that half of the fluids in it had long since passed their expiry date; and many of his instruments hadn't been sanitised.

Instantly I decided that if I got injured at any point during the next three weeks I'd try to use my own training to patch myself up. I didn't want him anywhere near me.

Things didn't improve when I met the short, round Jake. Almost the first thing he told me was that his uncle was high up at the security firm who were employing us. His eyes met mine meaningfully as he spoke. He clearly wanted me to understand the significance of this personal relationship with the bosses.

Maybe he wanted me to overlook the fact that his military experience hadn't gone past a few months' training in the UK, which he'd had to cut short for medical reasons. Funnily enough, he was much keener to talk about his uncle …

I'd have been able to overlook the nepotism if Jake hadn't also been all over the place. He emitted an absurdly powerful level of nervous energy. It was like he'd drunk 15 Red Bulls. I don't think I've ever met anyone so anxious and jittery. He could barely even open a door without having a flap. The worst thing was that his levels of panic were so constantly elevated that they spread quickly. Five minutes in a car with him and clients would feel as if the world was about to end.

I just felt sorry for him. Like Dylan he was in his thirties but had barely any experience. They'd come here for the money and found themselves in a situation that they weren't equipped to deal with.

My team was completed by Ben, a bloke from the West Country who was supposed to be my second in command, and who'd had two years in an infantry regiment as a driver in logistics, plus some time in the TAs. This might have been true, though if it was, I'm pretty sure he must have spent most of his service asleep. It was the vagueness that got me. When I asked what they'd been up to over the last couple of months, he said, sounding almost dazed, 'Oh, we just go out and do jobs.' For some reason he let Dylan and Jake, who I realised would mention his uncle's position to anybody, talk down to him.

But the tall, angular Ben was also pretty much the only member of my security detail who I even half-trusted, which says it all really.

By this stage, I wasn't expecting much from the vehicles we were going to be travelling in. Which is just as well, because they too were barely fit for purpose.

I trotted across to where I'd been told they were parked. There was an armoured pick-up, which would carry the Iraqis, and two armoured 4x4s, for the rest of us. I'd been hoping we'd be able to travel in something that didn't make us stand out – I'd already figured our best chance lay in blending in rather than drawing attention to ourselves. With these armoured monsters we'd inviting people to take an interest in us.

I wandered round them, like somebody looking at a second-hand car, occasionally moving closer to inspect a worrying piece of rust. I know next to nothing about anything mechanical, but it was obvious, even to me, that they were old, and that nobody had spent much effort maintaining them. All of them were missing important pieces from their breakdown kit, and though there were spare tyres, they were all worn and covered in cracks.

I turned round to speak to Dylan, Ben and Jake, who'd followed me to the garage. 'Have you done first parade?'

They looked at me blankly. 'Have you checked the vehicles? Are there spare tyres? What are the oil levels like? We're going to be driving miles and miles into bandit country. I don't want to break down. Do you?'

Nobody spoke. It was like each of them wanted somebody else to speak up and take the blame. I was used to working with people who'd served proper time in the special forces, not nuggets like these who'd worn a uniform for five minutes.

'OK,' I said, my heart sinking. 'Looks like we've got work to do.'

I started asking a few more questions, hoping against hope that maybe my initial impressions were misplaced. Maybe they were a more impressive outfit than I thought?

No. They all seemed unaware of even the most basic contact drills. Worse, they either refused to admit this, or just didn't seem to care.

The three of them stood there, bristling with resentment, suspicion, and beneath it all a small amount of shame. They clearly hated the fact that their deficiencies had been exposed. But I wasn't doing any of this for my own personal amusement. I just wanted to come back from this trip alive, ideally with all my limbs intact. If a few awkward conversations were the price of that, then so be it.

We had a few hours left before night fell. Not long, and yet I realised I had an opportunity to share something of what I knew. I rummaged around in my rucksack, eventually finding what I was looking for: a few magnetic buttons in different colours. I strode over to one of the vehicles and clamped the buttons onto its side, before beckoning Dylan, Jake and Ben over. They looked puzzled, though I was pleased to see that at the very least I'd grabbed their attention. I moved the buttons around to demonstrate how to execute a handful of rudimentary drills, like how our vehicles could move to support each other in the event of contact, or how we could move clients out of an immobilised vehicle and into one that could take them to safety.

They nodded along, and I think they took a fair amount of what I told them in. I began to feel frustrated, wishing that I had more time with them in which I could help make them competent operators. I offered a silent prayer to a god I don't believe in, hoping against hope that we'd manage to avoid trouble on this expedition. But even as I formed the words in my mind, I knew this was unlikely.

◻

Later that day, I discovered that our radios weren't working. In their place we were given a pair of satellite phones. This was a good idea in theory. The problem in practice was we were only given two scratchcards worth of credit, which I knew from experience would barely last a call. What good would that be if and when we got caught in an ambush? I tried to contact my bosses to see if there was any chance of getting any more minutes for our phone.

'Sorry, Mel, mate,' they said, not sounding the least bit apologetic, 'we'd like to help but there's no time.'

This was true, everything was being done at the last minute.

I thought: *This is insane.* In the last twenty-four hours I'd learned that none of my teams was capable of navigating their way out of a paper bag, and that their drills were hopeless. Their weapons were neither properly cleaned nor oiled. The Iraqis seemed like nice blokes, but they barely knew their left from their right. Only one of them spoke English, though he only translated for his mates at irregular intervals. This meant that most of the time when I asked a question, they'd cheerfully say, 'Yes, boss,' then stare expectantly at me, like toddlers waiting to be dressed.

Now this. We were about to head off into one of the most threat-filled stretches of territory on the planet, and to all intents and purposes we had no way of calling for help. *What on earth had I let myself in for?* For the next few days, every time I stopped for a moment, the same phrases buzzed away in the back of my mind. *This is insane. What am I doing here?*

I kicked myself for agreeing to this shambles.

The turd on the top of the cake of shit I'd been presented with was the two engineers we were going to be escorting. I heard them before I saw them. They were talking loudly in treacle-thick southern accents about Barack Obama, who was American president at the time. 'We don't want the guy,' one of the voices asserted, loudly. Something about his tone told me that the thing they objected to most of all was the colour of the president's skin.

This suspicion was confirmed when I saw the look of shock that briefly passed across their faces when they first laid eyes on me. I had a shock of my own: they both had AK-47s slung over their shoulders. This wasn't normal for a job like this, the clients weren't supposed to be *armed*. For what felt like the millionth time that day, I thought: *This is insane. What am I doing here?*

Mike and Creed, the American contractors, were physical opposites. Mike, another chain-smoker, was a big guy with a long, bushy beard and a belly that flopped over the band of his trousers. I grew to hate talking to him because when you did it meant having to look at the fragments of whatever he'd just eaten that clung to the springy hairs around his mouth. I'd rarely seen anyone so obviously unhealthy. His skin was covered in livid red blotches and he was always out of breath, every step he took looked like an effort. I was genuinely worried he'd have a heart attack before we returned to Baghdad.

Creed was tall, angular and thin. He resembled a coat-hanger in human form. What really got me about him was that he was constantly chewing tobacco, a habit I'd never liked. Seeing him swilling the disgusting brown slurry around his mouth reminded me of an American operator I'd once been out on the piss with. He'd spent the evening spitting his 'backy' into an empty beer bottle. Somewhere towards the end of the night, when I'd consumed just enough to seriously impair my judgement, I'd accidently taken a swig out of what I thought was Budweiser. That wasn't a mistake I was anxious to repeat.

I was grown-up enough to know that you don't have to fall in love with everyone you're assigned to protect. Still, I wasn't looking forward to spending a week with this pair of brash, abrasive rednecks. I was left almost speechless by the way they treated Iraqis, who they sniggeringly referred to as 'ragheads'. They were rude and abrupt with me, but they talked to the locals like they were the shit on the soles of their shoes.

Every second I spent in their company made me feel homesick for the warmth and support I'd encountered at CBS, and sympathy for the poor sods who had to work with people like this on a permanent basis.

I hated the way that this sort of experience ate away at my ability to trust others.

Everything was shitty, old and badly cared-for. Nobody cared about us. We were just figures on a balance sheet. Any corner that could be cut, would be. The men that were supposed to be helping protect the contractors were incompetent. They were drunks or fantasists; in at least one case they were both.

One of the things I'd liked most about the SAS was the trust that existed between us all. There was no need to check that the other blokes had done their jobs. We looked after each other, and if one of us fucked up, they'd always put their hand up and admit it. Now, though, I had to play the angry sergeant major with them, a role I wasn't comfortable with. I don't enjoy confrontation, I don't like yelling at people, but nor am I a massive fan of the idea of dying in a ditch because somebody else couldn't be bothered to clean their gun or check that our vehicle had fuel.

But I reckon I could have forgiven a fair amount of their incompetence had any of them possessed anything even resembling a sense of humour.

One of the things that connected us all in the regiment was a sense of humour: another of the values David Stirling insisted upon. To me, there's something really crucial about that ability to see the funny side, even in the darkest moments. Those sorts of jokes helped release tension, but they also gave us a chance to take a step *outside* the situation we were in, to gain a new perspective. The time during selection when I'd started pissing myself at the thought of Sammy's face was the bridge that took me across to a different mental position. I sometimes think, too, that having a sense of humour helps keep you in touch with your humanity. It's a generous, warm-hearted thing to be able to laugh at yourself or to share a funny moment with others. It binds you to each other.

Perhaps that was why it felt even more important to keep laughing, keep joking, when we were behind enemy lines. No matter how serious things seemed, we'd always take the piss. You didn't want to be the person who tripped over, or burned yourself, or indeed fouled up your mates' only meal of the day.

I remember one morning when we returned from an operation, all of us starving. We knew we were likely to be heading out again at any moment, so this was our one chance to get some food down us. It was my turn to cook, which shouldn't really have made much difference either, because we made our meals the same way most of us had ever since we'd joined the army. You slop all your rations together into one big pot, heat it up, then dig in with what we called our 'racing' spoons. You didn't need to be a cordon bleu chef to pull it off. In fact, on balance, it probably helped if your standards weren't too high.

I always carried some Jamaican hot sauce in my kit. If the food is shit, but you put in just a little bit of spice, that's a morale boost right there. This time, I'd also found some curry powder. I reckoned a bit of both the powder and the sauce would give the meal a bit more interest. I tipped a little in and stirred the pot.

I looked around; two pairs of hungry eyes stared back. I swear I heard a stomach rumble. 'Not long now, lads.'

Absent-mindedly I added a shake more hot sauce and another spoonful of curry powder. Then, just to be sure, I added a last few drops of spice. *They'll enjoy this,* I thought.

'OK, food's up.'

They scrambled across, looking excited. You really don't appreciate food properly until you've had a properly empty belly.

I turned away to tidy a couple of things up, listening to the chink and scrape as they helped themselves. There was even a murmur of appreciation. This didn't last long. 'Fucking *hell*, Mel, are you trying to fucking kill us?' I whipped round. Their faces were red, their eyes streaming, and they were all frantically tipping the contents of their water bottles down their throats.

Curious and slightly embarrassed, I dipped my own spoon in then raised it to my lips and took a slurp. *This is fine,* I thought. *What are they complaining about?* Then, a second later. *Bollocks.* It felt as if an IED had just detonated in my mouth. I started sweating uncontrollably, my stomach was screaming at me. *What have I done?*

All of this was made worse by the stream of abuse being unleashed on me by my mates, still steaming at the loss of their only chance for a feed. 'You twat, we're going out with empty stomachs because of you.'

I tried making the odd joke when I was around the other guys, hoping I'd be able to form some sort of bond, but they only seemed to laugh when they saw something bad happen to another human. So although there is nothing I love more than talking to people, finding out more about them, having a giggle, on this trip I found that I was keeping to myself.

¤

The job continued on its downward trajectory. The following morning we set off. Jake would be driving my vehicle, and Dylan would be behind the wheel of the other. I had the dubious privilege of sitting in front of the Americans. Winter had just begun and the air was chilly. I shivered and drew my thick North Face coat around me as we waited for the vehicles' heaters to kick into gear. Finally, they started pumping out hot air, which was pretty much the only thing about them that functioned as they were supposed to.

Over the next few hours, the two 4x4s and the Iraqis' armoured pick-up seemed to be taking it in turns to break down. One of the sickly sounding engines would sputter to a halt, then cough apologetically. The prompt for a frantic attempt to patch up vehicles that were just not fit for purpose.

Halfway through our journey, as we crossed a bridge that extended across a deep gulley, I asked Jake to stop. Without explaining what I was doing, I scrambled out and jogged to the bridge. I peered over its sides. *Yes*, I thought, *this is the same place.* For a few seconds, memories from years before crashed back into my mind. We'd been behind enemy lines and had found ourselves confronted by an overwhelming enemy force. I still don't know how we had escaped that night. I had sudden visions of the way that shells had exploded with a vicious, shattering thunder just metres from where I was standing right now. But any sign of what had happened then had long-since disappeared. As I made my way back to my 4x4, I tried to work out whether this encounter with my past was merely a coincidence, or something more: a warning, or an omen.

That night we stopped at an American military base the security company had stayed inside before. It was home to a full unit, perhaps 800 men as well as their vehicles. As we drove past the parked lines of Humvees, with their .50 machine guns sitting in a small embrasure on their roofs, I felt a stab of jealousy. *If only we had something like that.*

Still, all around us were signs of how embattled and threatened this small outpost in the middle of nowhere was. The base was ringed by blast walls, but almost every one of the prefab structures within the walls was surrounded by piles of sandbags.

We were staying in a bunch of Portakabins on the edge of the camp. This part of the base, home to the various contractors and translators that worked there, was muddy and dissolute. The toilets that serviced this section were an overflowing, stinking health hazard – which meant that locals simply squatted in the mud around them when they needed to empty their bowels.

It had begun to snow and the flimsy prefabs we'd be sleeping in provided precious little protection against the cold. Still, I settled into familiar routines, ones that I'd been following for the last two decades of my life, cleaning my weapons so that I could be sure they'd be ready if they were needed.

Almost reluctantly, I asked the other members of my team if I could check theirs. I knew what I was going to see before I'd even started looking. One of the Iraqis showed me his gun, it was caked in sand. 'Have you cleaned this?' 'Yes, boss.'

I called over to Dylan. His gun was just as filthy. *Jesus, what was wrong with these blokes?* I checked them all, one after the other, with mounting horror. How had they survived this long?

Later that night I trudged from our quarters to the gym I'd been told had been placed somewhere in the centre of the base. It was here, in this heated tent stuffed full of weights and running machines, that I met Captain Tom Kiernan. I'd always liked American officers, even the ones that arrived with that West Point sheen still clinging to them. They rarely seemed to be as stiff or stuck-up as their British equivalents could be. Captain Tom Kiernan was no different. He was tall, blond and friendly, with the sort of square-jawed good looks that made you wonder whether he was a Hollywood actor rather than a soldier. But there was something about his calm, brisk manner that inspired confidence in me. He struck me as the sort of bloke that you'd want by your side if things went south.

We were a nuisance in their eyes, rich contractors making money and potentially attracting trouble that we had no intention, and certainly no ability, to deal with ourselves. We'd got talking after he heard my British accent. I decided to tell him I'd served in the SAS. It's not really the done thing to talk, unprompted, about having been in the special forces. This time, though, I realised that it might have a value that went beyond securing another man's respect.

Then I'd watched as his eyes got wider as I explained what we were out here for. 'God, man, you're crazy.'

He told me as much as he could about the area we were going to be travelling to.

They only ever went out mobbed-up in big convoys of Humvees. The only defence we had was time. I figured if we avoided coming and going on a predictable routine and only stayed a couple of hours we could avoid attracting unwanted attention.

Captain Kiernan nodded. 'Whatever you do, make sure you leave before dark.'

'Oh yeah, 100 per cent.' It was good to talk to somebody who I felt was on the same page as me. And it was reassuring to know that there was at least one, fairly straightforward, thing we could do to preserve our safety.

I paused, trying to work out how he'd react to what I was about to ask. *Might as well try,* I thought, *what's the worst that could happen?* 'Look,' I said, 'I know this is asking a lot, but do you reckon if you'd be able to check up on us, only if you're already out on patrol in the same area to the building site we're going to.'

'Sure, man.'

I thanked him effusively and he looked a little embarrassed, as if it would have been more surprising if he *hadn't* agreed. But I knew that he was doing me a huge favour, and when I returned to our quarters, it was with a new spring in my step.

▢

I was sharing a room with the rest of the security detail, and the two American contractors were in by themselves. While they had heating provided by a big generator in their lodging, our accommodation was damp, cold and stank of mould. It was obvious that it hadn't been used for a while. The only warmth came from a small stove that sat in the middle of the room, though there was little firewood, and even that I'd had to beg from Captain Kiernan.

The sleeping arrangements had, inevitably, been a source of tension. Dylan had spluttered with horror when I told him we would be quartered alongside the Iraqis.

'Why are they in our room?' he demanded.

'Fuck off, Dylan, they're staying with us.'

Dylan pouted, then nodded miserably. It was almost a relief to know that somebody else was having as shit a time of it as I was.

Conscious that we had another big day ahead of us, I got my head down early, grateful that I'd brought with me a good sleeping bag from my time in the SAS. The Iraqis settled into the rough wooden cots around me, though for the moment, nobody turned out the light. Instead, they talked quietly, their breath pluming in the frigid air around us. I considered telling them to shut up, but the accumulated exhaustion and tension of the last few hours dragged me down. I slept deeply until at some point I was woken by a thump, followed by barely stifled giggles. I pulled myself upright, blearily trying to make out what was going on. There, in the corner of the room, lit by a torch, sat three of the Iraqis. The fourth member of their quartet stumbled between the sleeping bodies of the rest of the team, clearly woozy with drink. He was yelling something I didn't understand at that moment, though I would later learn that he'd run outside, convinced he'd seen genies. The sour-sweet smell of whisky drifted across to me. One of them must have sneaked it in.

I turned on the four pissed Iraqis. 'What the *fuck* are you doing? You do know what we're doing tomorrow? You do know that Al-Qaeda are swarming around exactly the area we're travelling to?' I grabbed the interpreter. 'Tell them that if a single drop of alcohol crosses any of their lips, at any point before we get back to Baghdad, I'll tell their manager.' He nodded, then spoke quickly to his mates.

They smiled at me, their unfocused eyes glinting in the room's half-light. 'Yes, boss!'

□

Our destination was an hour from the American base. The first section was easy, we were travelling on good tarmac roads. But after 30 minutes we had to turn off and drive for another half hour on dirt tracks that ran through a seemingly endless wilderness of sand and scrub.

The contractors were involved in building a factory or a water-treatment plant, or something like that, in the middle of the desert, and seemed to be preoccupied by rebars, a word I'd never heard before that appeared constantly in their conversations. That's as much as I knew. Normally, with clients you share a bit of your life and what you're doing; that's how you build a rapport. But they weren't that interested in talking to me. And after a few attempts at getting to know them, I realised I wasn't that bothered about finding out more.

The plant itself was in the early stages of construction. It didn't even have a fence around its perimeter. Although it was a government project, it wasn't guarded by any soldiers, instead there were a handful of Iraqis who moved busily around the piles of freshly dug earth, occasionally disappearing into the assorted prefab buildings that dotted the area.

We were some distance from the main road, far enough away that it was unlikely anybody would come here by accident. And yet throughout the first day we spent there I'd been noticing people approach the site in pick-ups. We'd been clocked.

My hackles rose as I tried to work out what they were doing. Were they just curious, or were they making a recce? There was no way of knowing if they were bad actors themselves, but even if they weren't, I knew that word of our presence would get around soon.

The next chance I got to catch up with Creed and Mike I shared my concerns with them.

'People know we're here. Before long, someone nasty is going to take an interest in us. We can't prevent that, we all know that. But we can do a few basic things to help.'

I explained that we needed to follow Captain Kiernan's advice. There was only one track in and out, so we had to make sure we left before dusk as well as staggering the times we came and went.

Mike responded with the insolence of a man who knew he held the power needed to get his own way.

'That's not going to happen, Mel. We're here to do a job. You're here to protect us, not get in our way.' His features arranged themselves into a wolfish smile. 'Phone your boss, see what he says.' He spat, revealing a row of uneven tobacco-stained teeth.

'Are you fucking crazy? You want to stay *here*?' I was struggling to contain myself. I was angry at him because he was endangering the lives of everyone on this building site. I was even angrier because there was nothing I could do, no authority I could appeal to. Sure, I could use our entire supply of phone credit to call my bosses on the satellite phone, but I knew, just as well as Mike and Creed knew, that I'd be reminded who was paying our company money. It had always been made clear to us that if the clients said 'Jump', the only realistic response was for us to ask, 'How high?'

We were hundreds of miles from anywhere that the local police could even pretend to be in control of, and the American military camp was sixty minutes' drive away. A lot of very bad things can happen to you in an hour. And we were civilians who had come here under our own steam, for our own reasons – those soldiers had no formal obligation to protect us.

Just by being there we had compromised ourselves.

By this point, everybody knew about the chaos and bloodshed that had followed in the insurgency's wake. Every day seemed to bring new horror stories of murders and kidnappings. But I honestly don't believe that Mike and Creed thought that *they* would be the ones that found themselves in trouble. I reckoned too that they thought that somehow the fact of them carrying assault rifles, and having had the experience of ripping into the Alabama wildlife on hunting trips back home, would be enough to protect them if the bad thing did end up happening.

Every day we had the same struggle. No matter how hard I tried to persuade them otherwise, they insisted on leaving the American base at the same time every morning, and staying at the building site for as long as they possibly could. But somehow, though we always seemed to be shadowed by mysterious figures, we seemed to be living charmed lives. Maybe, I thought, the watchers were just interested locals, or petty thieves hoping to make off with some unattended machinery. Captain Kiernan had been as good as his word. He might come just once a day, his column of vehicles might not even stop, but he'd always come. The only time they hadn't been able to, he come by our accommodation to apologise. Perhaps his presence alone was enough to intimidate anyone considering attacking us.

By the fourth day, Creed and Mike seemed to have become even more complacent. As they busied themselves inspecting potential locations for buildings and talking, as always, about rebars (fair play to those lads, whatever their other flaws, they had a real passion for concrete-reinforcing steel) I carried on staring into the wilderness around us. Forever trying to make out whether the shapes I could occasionally see flickering in the distance were anything I needed to worry about. I'd been troubled ever since we'd arrived that morning and discovered that none of the local Iraqis were present on site. What did they know that we didn't? Or was it just a coincidence? I felt the same jangly mix of anticipation and fear I'd experienced as a young soldier sitting in a cramped, stinking bivouac in South Armagh. I thought: *At least this time round I'm dry.*

The hours ticked by. At some point late that afternoon I looked up at the sky. The sun was starting to dip, the shadows cast by the unfinished factory were beginning to lengthen. It was time for us to return.

I ambled over to Mike and Creed, who were deep in discussion about what I guessed was a thorny engineering issue. 'OK, guys, it's time we were on the move.'

Creed looked up at me and spat a great gobbet of tobacco into the sand a couple of feet away from where we stood. It landed with a wet plop and I felt the little pulse of revulsion this act always inspired in me.

'We ain't done,' he said, in the voice he usually reserved for Iraqis who'd annoyed him.

'I'm sorry,' I said, 'that's not an option. We can't stay here, it's too dangerous.'

Creed stared at me for a couple of beats. I could see his cheek twitch and redden, like he was trying to control his temper.

'You're not listening to me, Mel.' Then he slowed, for emphasis. 'We. Are. Not. Leaving. We're staying here for as long as it takes. If we have to stay the night, we stay the night.'

'OK, one hour. We can stay another hour. But we have to leave before last light.' They grunted assent, like they'd made a huge concession to me. I was left feeling even more anxious than before. Nothing about this was right. Surely we were pushing our luck by staying this long? And yet I knew how flimsy my authority was. I could hardly force them to leave at gunpoint.

The sky continued to darken, and I continued to scan the horizon. Then, fifty or so minutes later, as the two Americans conducted what they claimed was one last check round the site, I spotted vehicles.

At first they were just a few specks haloed by a fuzzy cloud of dust. As they came closer I could use my binoculars to help me pick out individual vehicles. Six of them. White SUVs and pick-ups with big .50 calibre Dushka machine-guns on the back.

Occasionally they'd disappear for a few seconds as they swooped into a dune, before emerging, their windscreens flashing red in the fading sun.

I carried on staring through my binoculars, hoping desperately that sooner rather than later I'd be able to make out something that indicated that they were Iraqi military. Any faint, irrational hopes I'd been nurturing were exploded once they opened fire. I could see the men themselves swathed in black clothing that was supposed to put the fear of God into whatever enemy they faced. Their rifles spat tracer into the sky above us. For the moment, there was little danger of being hit – their barrage was too erratic and poorly aimed for that – but it was clear that we didn't have long before we'd be in serious danger.

Mike and Creed's faces were masks of disbelief. They both stood there, rooted to the spot, as if they couldn't believe that this was actually happening. I found myself wishing that I had just one old pal from the regiment standing beside me. Creed, Mike, Ben, Dylan, Jake and the Iraqis were as much use as a pile of empty suitcases.

'Move!' I screamed, breaking into their stupor. 'MOVE! MOVE!' I gestured frantically at our vehicles. As we sprinted across the sand, the crackle of gunfire from behind us grew louder.

The four members of our Iraqi security detail, who were standing on the back of a pick-up, shouldered their rifles and the air around us began to fill with sharp cracks and the stench of carbine. I looked around again. Everyone from our party had scrambled into the two 4x4s we'd travelled here in. Disbelief had given way to animal terror.

Our 4x4 lurched forward, before quickly picking up pace. Thankfully the problems that had afflicted it on the way out seemed to be under control. I looked back into the rear of the vehicle. Mike and Creed sat motionless, their faces drained of any colour, their eyes bright with fear. Terror had turned them into rigid statues and the weapons they'd spent the last few days brandishing with such bloodthirsty intent now lay untouched by their feet alongside a reeking pile of vomit.

Our only hope of surviving was to get out as quickly as we could. I reckoned if we could make it to the tarmacked road a few kilometres away we'd be able to outpace them. The problem was that we needed to negotiate a 30-minute scramble along a sandy half-track at speed.

We bumped and rumbled for a kilometre or two. Then, just as I peered into our rear-view mirror to see if we'd managed to put any distance between us and our pursuers, we plunged down into a hollow filled with soft sand. We stopped abruptly, as if someone had slammed the handbrake on. The 4x4's engine roared, straining in a futile attempt to escape. *Fuck. Fuck. Fuck.* Then there was the little refrain that had been spinning through my head for the last week. *This is insane. What am I doing here?*

The insurgents were closer now. Scenting blood, they had opened fire again.

I leaped out of our vehicle and started sending some rounds back in their direction. I could see the men who were trying to hunt us down: they were standing on the backs of their pick-ups, or hanging out of their SUVs' windows. Bullets thudded into the sand around us, a few even landed with a sharp metallic ping on our vehicles.

Alongside this came the growl of another engine. I whipped round just in time to see the pick-up with its cargo of four Iraqi guards speeding off, away from where we were stranded. I thought about calling after them, before realising that this would do no good, beyond giving me a chance to vent my anger and frustration. I cursed myself: *Why hadn't I insisted on going earlier?*

Behind me, the second 4x4 had stopped, Dylan and Ben had opened their doors. I looked back, expectantly, ready to direct their covering fire. But they both stood stock still, their mouths agape. Panic etched onto their faces. Like Mike and Creed, they seemed to be struggling to process the fact that *this* was happening to them. I let off another burst, then ducked down to reload and yell at Dylan and Ben. 'Lads, MOVE!' Still they hesitated as bullets slammed into my 4x4's hide. I needed their firepower if our driver was going to stand any chance of reversing out of the sand that had locked our front wheels in a grip as tight as any vice.

It was just at that moment that a glint in the distance signalled another group of vehicles was approaching. They were coming from the opposite direction, cutting off our line of retreat. *God, I thought, so this is how it ends?*

All I could think was. *We are dead. We are dead.* There seemed to be no way out of this. We were either going to be butchered out there in the open, or kidnapped. Both fates were equally grim. What I hated most was the idea that I was going to be killed because a pair of pig-headed idiots had refused to listen to me, and I'd not had the authority to make them see sense. When news of my demise reached home, I wouldn't be celebrated as a hero defending my country, I'd just be seen as a mercenary who'd bitten off more than he could chew.

My head filled with thoughts of Zoe and the kids. Our gamble had failed. Zoe was going to be left a widow with a big mortgage that she had no way of paying off. *Fuck. FUCK.*

The vehicles that had been chasing us drew steadily closer. I found myself wondering aimlessly which of the two parties was going to have the best chance to catch us.

I shaded my eyes, trying to make out who was standing between us and a chance at escape. Was that a Humvee? For a couple of seconds I didn't dare to believe what I'd seen. Or had I just thought I'd seen it? I knew as well as anyone that both the desert and desperation can play tricks on you. No, it was a Humvee. And another. The cavalry was coming to rescue us.

Relief flooded my body. It was almost enough for me to bundle Mike and Creed into a celebratory bear hug. We were saved.

The column continued to eat up the ground beneath it, thundering towards us. Their big .50s started booming, sending a hail of bullets towards the men who only minutes before had been closing in on what they must have thought was a guaranteed kill. Quickly realising that they were outmatched, they had all made 180-degree turns and were speeding frantically away from us, pursued by another volley from the Americans, who pulled up beside us in a flurry of dust and sand.

Captain Kiernan leaped out of his vehicle, smiling broadly. I moved towards him: 'You've saved our lives.' I meant it, we'd have been carrion without him and his men.

'How did you end up staying so late out here?' he asked. I explained what had happened. Instantly his expression shifted. He pushed past me, towards the two pale, sweaty contractors who had climbed out of our vehicles. As Kiernan approached, they suddenly had the look of two naughty schoolboys who'd been caught with their hands in the tuck box.

The American officer delivered a performance for the ages, tearing into Mike and Creed, who stood there heads bowed, mutely accepting their punishment. He pointed at me: 'Do you think he's an idiot?'

'No,' they both mumbled.

'What's that?' Kiernan cupped his hand around his ear, 'I didn't hear you.'

'No.'

'So fucking listen to him, otherwise you guys are going to get yourself killed.'

They slunk off back into the 4x4. If they'd had tails, they'd have been between their legs. Captain Kiernan grinned at me. I beamed back, giddy at the idea that, somehow, I was still alive.

ロ

Creed and Mike never mentioned what had happened, and the argument we'd had about staying. Nor did I. I thought about rubbing it in a bit. Who doesn't like being proved right like that? But I also thought: *What's the point?*

The job lasted for another week. The two contractors were notably quieter and less arrogant, though I wondered how long that new gentleness would last. We made just one more run out to the building site, a visit that barely lasted an hour. Then I went back to CBS, unbelievably relieved, but also wondering how much longer I was willing, or able, to do this sort of work.

EPILOGUE
THIS IS ALL WE'VE GOT

In August 2005, just a few months after I'd arrived in Baghdad, New Orleans and much of the area around it was devastated by Hurricane Katrina.

The news broke as I was landing back in Britain. ABC, another media company on the roster of the security firm who employed me, was sending a team; they wanted me to go. So I only had time to give Zoe a kiss and a bundle of washing before I turned round and caught a flight to the US.

The poorest areas had been hit hardest. There were rumours that the levee had been deliberately sabotaged to ensure that it was the Lower Ninth Ward, not the prosperous downtown, that bore the brunt of the disaster. When we told the police that we were heading for these areas they tried to warn us off. There had been looting, they said. In fact, they told us, they avoided going there after dark at any time. But that was where the story was.

Our little boat puttered away through water that slopped in and out of the tops of houses. Here and there we saw people still sitting on their balconies, defiant: 'I'm not leaving my building,' they'd tell us when we asked why they had not left. 'This is all we've got.'

In other places, obese corpses, bloated by heat, their arms the size of rubber dinghies, floated past us. Other bodies had been caught, in ludicrous positions, in trees. The revolting swamp water that had rushed into the city was polluted further by petrol that had escaped from submerged gas stations. Sometimes you'd see bubbles on the surface: another gallon of petrol trying to escape the gloom below.

All over, people waded through waist-high water like zombies. A lot of them were on drugs, or cut up. These were desperate human beings. Some of them had robbed Walmarts. But they'd run out of food and drinkable water. What else could they do? They were in the richest, most modern country on the planet. The leader of the free world. And it had gone to pot in three days. A few of the locals were shooting at helicopters. When we asked them why, they said, 'What have they done for us? They've rescued dogs but they left us behind. They're not even giving us water.'

I remember the humidity, I remember our excitement at being among the first – if not *the* first – people to get hold of a boat, and I remember the strange sense, almost like vertigo, of going back in time.

It wasn't just the way that the water had stripped away so many elements of modern existence, but the fact that we suddenly appeared to be surrounded by bands of 'good ol' boys'. These men who seemed to have sprung fully formed from a version of America's South that I thought had disappeared years ago.

After we'd been there a couple of days there was an influx of sheriffs and deputies. They all seemed excited by the chance all the chaos gave them. 'Yeah, man! Yeah, boy!' Their rule was that if anyone was looting it was legitimate to kill them. But their definition of looting felt very loose to me. They were just lynching gangs with fancy badges.

One of their boats came past us, a small RIB, carrying a dozen of them, bristling with weapons, in all-round defence. I thought, *What are these guys doing?* They were bellowing at terrified people: 'Get out of your house! Get out of your house! Get out of your fucking house!' They weren't helping; they were just contributing to the chaos of those days.

A little later I saw what was left of two Black boys, no more than 14 or 15, who'd been killed. One was naked from the waist up. The second was covered by a bloodied sheet.

Each of them had the possessions they'd saved from the water wrapped up in another sheet that they'd then hoisted over their shoulders, like Dick Whittington. That was enough – in the eyes of those good ol' boys – to mark them as looters.

The strange thing was they'd been shot to pieces but there weren't any shell cases. I started to look for the firing point. Eventually I found it a hundred metres away. The ground there was carpeted with rounds from a .556 Armalite assault rifle and a couple of other calibres. Whoever had fired had now vanished. I could imagine what had happened. The two boys would have been shouted at by men carrying rifles. They would already have been scared and disorientated. Maybe they'd lost family members already. Certainly their whole lives had been swept away. So they'd have started running. Seconds later those white guys would have pulled the trigger, again and again and again.

But there was real heroism too. The person that stood out for me was an old Black guy, who must have been in his seventies. He told us that he wasn't leaving, then gestured at a number of rooftops that he'd smashed open in an attempt to rescue his neighbours. People were trapped in their attics – it was the only place they'd been able to run to when the levee broke in the early hours. 'We all said,' he told us, 'that if anything happens, we would look out for each other. That's all I'm doing.' Then he pointed to another corpse in a tree: 'He was my neighbour. I know everybody in that house; they're all dead. The water just went straight in.'

I don't know why the emergency services weren't going from house to house with their helicopters, checking every single rooftop. All he had was a tiny little rowing boat.

We returned the next day and he'd rescued a couple more people. But his face was drained, full of anxiety. 'I've not heard from my daughter. I don't know where she is, or what's happened to her. Make sure my daughter's all right, please.' Someone at ABC helped find her. We were able to cover the moment they were reunited. We saw his tears of joy.

◻

I'm mentioning my experiences in New Orleans now, at the end of the book, because to me those days, as well as being tragic, illustrate so much of what I've learned over my life.

There's the bad. Not just that human beings are so vulnerable – to both man-made and natural disasters – but that these times of stress can drag the worst in us out. We're all living on the precipice of a volcano, although nobody wants to admit it. People don't realise that these sorts of things can happen again. Chaos, misery: it's only a couple of days away. There's such a thin layer of skin between the two. People turn on people. People, specifically, turn on minorities.

But there is also the good. I was inspired by that old guy's love for his daughter, his desire to help both his community and a host of people he'd probably never met before. He had the same decency and bravery that I've been lucky to see in so many people, from blokes I've fought alongside to civilians like Larry Doyle. There was dignity, too. He wasn't willing to let his humanity be washed away in the flood.

I saw something similar around this time in Darfur, where I'd escorted a delegation of teenagers visiting the refugee camps for the UN's World Food Programme. I remember how cruel the conditions were, how much the people crammed into those camps were suffering. At one point I watched little kids drawing pictures of the men on camels, or leaning from helicopters, who had tormented them and their families.

Yet I also remember that amid all that misery and filth, they were always cleaning their teeth. They'd found a little bit of the river where they could wash their clothes. They invited me inside their neat huts where they shyly offered me food.

Their pride remained. No amount of cruelty or hardship could take that core of humanity away.

It's stuff like that that I cling on to when I fear that life is getting too bleak.

¤

I'd need that sort of reminder time and again for the last two years of my stint in Iraq.

After Baghdad, our family took another gamble, settling in Dubai for over a decade while I trained the UAE's special forces. We were safe and happy there; my two kids grew into wonderful human beings. Zoe trained as a teacher, while somehow making everything in our lives run. Every time I think I've learned what she's capable of, she shows me something new.

Then, in 2021, as the pandemic raged throughout the world, I took on a challenge I'd never expected I'd see myself doing in a million years: I went on television. I'd been vaguely aware of *SAS: Who Dares Wins* while I'd been out in Dubai, because a couple of my mates were on the show. When the producers approached me, I was hesitant at first, but we were planning on returning to Britain, and my contract with the UAE military was coming to an end. I thought, *Why not?* One other factor that influenced my decision was the wave of protest and controversy that had been unleashed by the death of George Floyd in May 2020. I never wanted to see Britain going back to days of race riots, with the National Front marching through the streets. I hoped I'd be able to share a positive message.

I always knew I'd only be on there for a short while, so I treated it like every new experience. You throw yourself into it, take the good and the bad, then move on.

For a number of reasons, I don't think I ever felt quite at home on screen. In one sense you're like an actor playing a role; it's not a medium where you can just be yourself.

I remember one day the producers on the show asked me to be more aggressive. 'You're too nice. That's what we're worried about.'

'Well,' I said, 'I can be aggressive. You want to see that? I'm not sure you really want me to be aggressive.'

'Can you swear?'

This I could do. I'm not actually a big one for swearing. I won't swear when I go home. Zoe swears more than I do, and she's nobody's idea of a potty mouth. I hate it when my kids do it. But it's something I do and have done in certain environments. I've been an instructor, I've beasted people, I know what it's like.

So I did what they wanted me to do, or at least what I *thought* they wanted me to do. The next day they came to see me again.

'I think you went a bit far, Melvyn. You can't call people this, you can't call people that.'

'Oh. What do you *want*?'

☐

I was also bothered by the idea that putting my head above the parapet like this could expose me and my family to those figures from my past who I feared might want to get revenge. At the same time, I had this crazy fear that there would be problems because I was still technically employed by the UAE's special forces while I was filming. I had visions of them cancelling my work visa and booting my family out as soon as they found out.

I'd seen similar punishments handed out for what I thought were minor infractions. All of this inhibited me, so I don't think I ever showed the best of myself. Which is a shame, because it's a great show. The producers are really impressive and I had lots of fun catching up with old mates like Billy Billingham and meeting all the SBS boys. It was great to see how members of the public responded to living in such stripped-back, minimalist conditions and pushing themselves to their limits and beyond. I'd leap at the chance to have another go.

¤

Other things were changing too. In early 2023 my mum died, taken in the end by dementia. After she'd retired, without my dad there, she went into herself. My brother and I wanted her to sell her house and move into a retirement community. But she said, 'No, I'd have to pay rent.' She could have had a community and played bingo whenever she wanted. Instead she lived as a recluse for 20 years. Still, given everything she had been through, there was something really impressive about the way she had found a way of existing that worked for her.

She carried on saving from her pension. She wouldn't even put the heating on. Like my dad, she was willing to go without because she wanted to leave as much as she could for us. Delroy and I would say, 'We don't need the house, Mum. We don't need the inheritance. We just want you to be happy.'

I'd always been sad that Dad never got to meet Amy and Sam. But Mum adored them, and they loved her. Even if she insisted on feeding them the kinds of things that were beginning to seem unhealthy even when I was a kid. 'Mum, it's dripping on toast! It's pure fat!' 'Mum, it's a family bag of Jelly Babies.'

'Well, it never bothered you.'

ロ

The changes in my life have given me more time and space to reflect than I've ever had before.

My life has its shadows, just as everyone's does.

Every night I wake Zoe by thrashing around in my sleep. She tells me that before I manage to drop off, I start shaking. Then, when I've entered deep sleep I will start to kick and punch, as if I'm fighting an invisible adversary.

When I wake, I do not feel upset; I remember only fragments of the nightmares that clearly torment me when I'm unconscious. Occasionally I'm shooting an enemy, or locked in close combat. Sometimes it's stuff that has happened, at other times it's things that I feared but escaped, like being held captive, or my parachute failing to open.

The things I've been through have re-wired me, I know that. They spent millions making me somebody who could deal with any threat, and nothing de-programming me.

I cannot walk along a normal city street without my eyes flicking up to upper storeys to establish whether there are any snipers watching. If I go into a station, or airport, I'll have a vivid sense of how I'd disarm and kill the terrorist who I'm afraid is there, waiting to commit an atrocity. Just like my dad, when I go into a pub I sit with my back to the wall, having worked out how I'd exit in the event of an emergency.

My past is clearly churning inside me.

I've had mates killed. I've had people shot right in front of me. I've seen bodies ripped to pieces by a car bomb. Too many of my friends have taken their own lives. I've had bombs dropped on me and been fired at by anti-aircraft guns, I've grappled hand to hand with terrorists. If I mentioned all my close escapes, this book would be a thousand pages long.

And through it all, I've just pushed it to the back of my mind. My attitude was always: *Bang, carry on with the job. Bang, carry on with life. Bang, carry on. It's over. That's done.* Part of that was because that the pace of combat did not allow for too much thinking. Even when people standing right by you are hit, or a round fizzes millimetres away from your skull, or you lose someone, you don't get to reflect about it until a long while afterwards. You only have one priority: go again.

I have made a habit of not talking about stuff that I really should. There have been times when I've been struck down by deep depression. I've been tormented by my nightmares and the conviction that I've let my family down. I've had days when I've failed to get out of bed, or sat in a dark room, desperate for Zoe to come home from work.

I don't know whether sharing something of this with others would have stopped these feelings, but I know it would have softened their impact and helped those around me understand why this positive, happy man was suddenly struggling so badly. I'd urge anyone who has experienced anything similar to open up, to treat their mental health as something that needs as much care as any other part of their body. It's OK to ask for help. Nobody gives medals to people because they suffered alone.

Still, most days the most overwhelming emotion I feel is gratitude. I am an extremely lucky man.

I was never academic at school. I couldn't think of anything worse than sitting in an office all day. That's not a dig at people who do – it's just I know myself well enough to understand that I'd really struggle in that environment.

Instead, I got to do a job I loved, serving the country I love. It took me around the world, taught me vast amounts and gave me the chance to meet amazing people. If I could do it again I would, in a flash, even taking into account all of the trauma.

At the end of it all, I'm content with what I have: a wife and kids that I love to bits, a nice home. Lots of good mates. To be honest, I don't need much else. I'm not bothered about money. I'm not into material things. I can settle anywhere. I've eaten at the same table as billionaires and people who have nothing. But after a couple of days of living it up I remember that I prefer beans on toast. I'm just a jeans-and-T-shirt kind of bloke.

I have no regrets in life, apart from bottling up so many of my darker experiences. I'd never pretend to be perfect; I've never been an angel. At the same time, I've never done anything malicious. I can't remember ever setting out to deliberately hurt someone for the sake of it. I've taken people's lives, and I know that there are always going to be people who disagree with that. But I was always confident that there was a good reason for what I was doing. Because, sadly, we don't live in a cotton-wool world. There are genuinely nasty people on this planet that have to be stopped. Sometimes fire has to be fought with fire. And I never pulled the trigger if I didn't have to.

I think I'm a good person, I've certainly tried to be. I'm lucky to have had a dad who set me such a strong example. I still think about him almost every day. Sammy Downes was a humble man from a humble background who set me up for the world. He wouldn't have had any idea about David Stirling's ethos – humility, integrity, humour, classlessness and the unrelenting pursuit of excellence – and yet he was a living demonstration of all those values. Dad never pretended life would be easy. At the same time, he was desperate that I would go out there and get the most I possibly could from it.

I reckon I've done that. I'm really proud to have gone from being a scared kid on a tough council estate – someone who was chased home by racist bullies and written off by teachers – to a man who reached the pinnacle of what was possible in the British Army. Along the way, there have been many challenges and a lot of drama. At times I've had to draw on all of David Stirling's principles as well as the example set by my dad just to keep going. I've had to learn the hard way that sometimes the biggest battles we all face are in our own heads. But I've come through. I've always stood my ground. I'm still smiling, I'm still excited about what the future might hold.

And if I was going to add anything to David Stirling's list, I'd say this: if you have the right mindset, if you look at the world in a positive way, there is no limit to what you can achieve.

ACKNOWLEDGEMENTS

I owe so much to so many people. But I'm especially grateful to Paddy McGuinness. Without him I would never have written this book.

Thank you, Larry Doyle, former CBS News bureau chief. An inspirational man who embodies David Stirling's ethos.

There is also my old boss from the Staffords. He helped me believe in myself and gave me the confidence to go for selection.

Huge thanks to Lorna Russell, Michelle Warner and all the team at Ebury, as well as to Amanda Harris and Elise Middleton at YMU.

I would like to thank all those who have served or are serving their country, including the emergency services. And I want to mention all the genuine, good, positive people of the world who have battled and are battling adversity. I know you will find a way through.

Finally, thank you to Mum and Dad, who gave me their resilience and made me realise the importance of never backing down. I think about you every day.